DIY FOR PRISONERS

By Tanner George Cummings

REVISED EDITION 2019
This publication has been revised to be in accordance with the
Board Policy, 03.91, Uniform Offender Correspondence Rules and
Regulations of the Texas Department of Criminal Justice.

FREEBIRD
PUBLISHERS

Freebird Publishers
Box 541, North Dighton, MA 02764
Info@FreebirdPublishers.com
www.FreebirdPublishers.com

Copyright © 2019 DIY For Prisoners
By Tanner George Cummings

Publisher & Distributor: Freebird Publishers
Box 541 North Dighton, MA 02764
Web: FreebirdPublishers.com
E-Mail: diane@freebirdpublishers.com
Toll-Free: 888-712-1987
Phone/Text: 774-406-8682
Send Letters to the Editor to the above address

ISBN-13: 978-0-9980361-6-8

ISBN: 0-9980361-6-1

Printed in the United States of America

ACKNOWLEDGEMENTS

First, I would like to thank the convicts from long ago who started coming up with these useful ideas, also the ones who made them into reality, and those who passed down the how-to knowledge through the generations.

I would also like to thank my editor, Ms. Joanne, for taking this project on and again turning my written words into masterpieces of easy-to-read, easy-to-understand, and easy-to-follow step-by-step instructions. Freebird Publishers earned much thanks too, for accepting my book and producing what you now hold in your hands.

And finally, I must thank my readers. It is people like you who push me to compile and complete works like this how-to guide. I hope this gives you a glimpse of the inner workings of prison life.

A NOTE FROM THE AUTHOR

Even if you are not a convicted felon, after you learn these how-to helpers that prisoners do and try the recipes from *The Cell Chef Cookbook* and *The Cell Chef Cookbook II* both available at Amazon and Freebird Publishers, then you will know what is like to live like a convict.

To be correct here, prisoners have redefined the term "convict." To be a convict is to be able to think outside (while being inside) the box. A convict must learn what can be substituted for something that they don't have and how to make something, or do something, with the available items they can get (either with or without permission).

I've learned that convicts are not feared simply because of the crimes they commit, but for the eagerness, willingness, and motivation to cross whatever boundaries necessary to meet their desires. This is also how human beings have advanced so far, by breaking down boundaries. These are the very boundaries that are deemed rebellious, unlawful and unusual just to name a few. If no one broke these boundaries down, then we would still be speculating and guessing what was on the other side.

DISCLAIMER

The views, thoughts, and opinions expressed in the text belong solely to the author and are not necessarily those of the publisher.

The information provided in this book is designed to provide helpful information on the subjects discussed. This book is not meant to be used, nor should it be used, as an electrical, medical, hygienic, or any other type of authoritative reference. It is sold with the understanding that the publisher is not engaged to render any type of professional advice.

No warranties or guarantees are expressed or implied by the publisher's choice to include any of the content in this volume. Neither the publisher nor the author shall be liable for any physical, psychological, emotional, financial, or commercial damages, including, but not limited to, special, incidental, consequential or other damages. References are provided for informational and entertainment purposes only. Our views and rights are the same: You are responsible for your own choices, actions, and results.

While best efforts have been used in preparing this book, the author and publisher make no representations or warranties of any kind and assume no liabilities of any kind with respect to the accuracy or completeness of the contents and specifically disclaim any implied warranties of merchantability or fitness of use for a particular purpose. Neither the author nor the publisher shall be held liable or responsible to any person or entity with respect to any loss or incidental or consequential damages caused, or alleged to have been caused, directly or indirectly, by the information or directions contained herein.

TABLE OF CONTENTS

MAKE A BAR OF SOAP

Required Supplies

- ✓ 15 bars of state soap (bar size is approx. 40 mm x 30 mm x 5 mm)
- ✓ 2-3 bottles caps of shampoo (optional)
- ✓ 1-3 bottle caps of water (may need more or less. you will have to use your judgment on the amount of water to use)

Makes one big bar of soap approximately 85-90 mm long, 55 mm wide, and 25-30 mm thick, should fit into a soap dish.

There are various ways of crushing the soap up: using a cup, your fingers, bowls, spoons, are just a few. Personally, use your fingers, thumbs, and the ground to crush up all 15 bars of soap.

Steps

1. Crush up all 15 bars of soap into a powdery form. Try to eliminate all lumps, as much as possible.

2. When soap is all crushed up, push all the soap into a circular pile. Push the center out to create a small crater ring pile.

3. Add your caps of water (and shampoo, if you desire).

4. Push all sides of the soap ring into the center and mash together. Press down, and with your hands sliding against the floor, press together the soap. Repeat a few times and then you can pick it up in your hands. Mash the soap together in your hands every way you can until the bar is solid and hard.

5. Toss down on a hard, flat surface, on all sides. Start to form a rectangular shape. (use a soap dish to gauge the length, width, and height of the soap bar).

6. Once the bar is in its final form, set it up somewhere that it won't be disturbed, for at least a day or two, to dry out some of the water.

You can also make bleach bars of soap by replacing the water in Step 3 with liquid bleach. However, if you have it, you should use dry liquid bleach (DLB) instead. It's recommended using only one or two heaping tablespoons of the DLB, because it's strong. Put them into a cup and add two or three caps of hot water, stir until all the DLB is completely dissolved, and use it in Step 3 in place of the water.

Another option is to simply pour the one to two heaping tablespoons of DLB into the center of the ring, then add the caps of hot water and proceed to the next step. By doing it this way, the soap will dry with a whitish green powdery look. Personally, do not like or use this method to make bleach bars of soap.

When using a bar, prefer using it standing on the ends to decrease the length and then rotate it with every use. So far have never found a way to use the bar without it eventually falling apart if you use it lying on its side only.

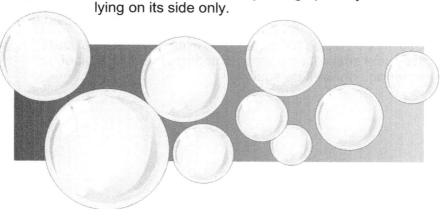

MAKE LIQUID SOAP

Required Supplies

- ✓ 10 bars of state soap or 6 bars of Dial soap or
- ✓ 7 bars of state soap (crushed/broken down)
- ✓ 3 bars of Dial soap (crushed/broken down)
- ✓ 1 clear plastic bottle (use a squeeze-cheese bottle)
- ✓ Boiling hot water
- ✓ Towel
- ✓ Shampoo

Steps

1. Crush up or break up the bars of soap.
2. Put all of the crushed up and broken-down bars of soap into the clean bottle.
3. Pour in the boiling hot water into the bottle until about 90% full.
4. Replace the lid on the bottle, ensure it is on tightly, wrap the towel around the bottle and shake until you see and hear all the soap completely dissolved in the liquid
5. (Optional) Add only 80% boiling hot water in step 3 then add some shampoo, if you like, and proceed to step 4.

Usually add a little bit of shampoo every time use the liquid soap and shake it up again. Sometimes add a little bit of hot water and shake it up again.

OTHER USES OF JARS AND BAGS

Of course, jars are useless after we finish the contents, or are they? No! They are not totally useless. Jars come in handy for many uses. Here is a list of a few:

- ♨ A drinking cup for water, cocoa, milk, etc.
- ♨ A pen or pencil holder
- ♨ A coffee mug
- ♨ A storage container for miscellaneous things
- ♨ Cut up pickles and jalapenos and other food in
- ♨ Cook soup in it
- ♨ Make homemade sauces in it

- ♨ Put your pet spider in in
- ♨ Clean your paint brushes in it
- ♨ Use as a snot cup
- ♨ Use to mix items (Good) (Condiments)

Chip bags are another reusable item. Here is a list of a few:

- ♨ Send hot water to other people.
- ♨ To cook spreads in
- ♨ To pass cooked food inside. Check out other books by author, *The Cell Chef Cookbook* and *The Cell Chef Cookbook II* at Amazon or FreebirdPublishers.com
- ♨ Cook pizzas in (Tdja Pizza)

Soup wrappers are good for the following:

- Put shots of drinks in
- Put chips, cookies, beans, rice, etc. in
- To make homemade tamales
  (Recipe in *The Cell Chef Cookbook*)

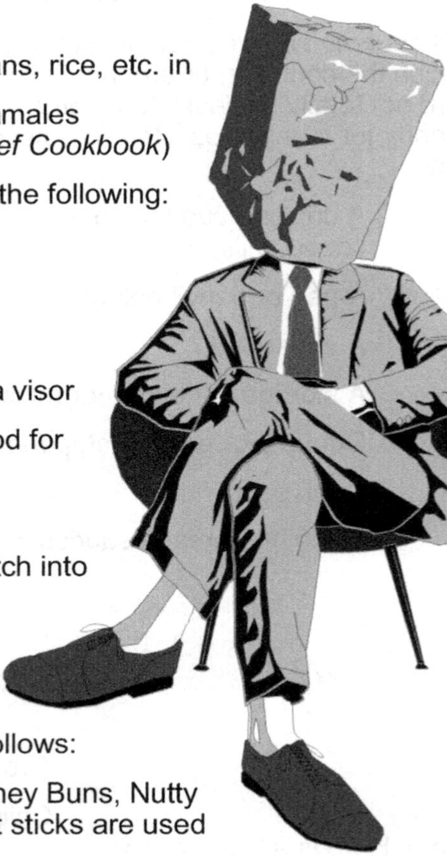

Shampoo bottles are good for the following:

- Drinking bottle
- Creating a speaker
- Pen or pencil jar
- Cut and use in hat for a visor

Heavy-duty trash bags are good for the following:

- Cooking in
- Cut into strips and stretch into long lines
- Wash in
- Put trash in

Additional items are used as follows:

- The wrappers from Honey Buns, Nutty Bars, Dunkin Doughnut sticks are used in different art projects.
- Foot tubes are good to cook and bake in.
- The self-serve cereal bowls are good to bake in.
- Rice bags are good to bring food back from the kitchen.
- Rice bags are also good to cook food in the hot pot with.

MAKE A HOMEMADE I.D. HOLDER

Required Supplies

- ✓ 2 tongues from state boots
- ✓ Sewing thread
- ✓ 1 black marker
- ✓ 1 sewing needle
- ✓ 1 ID holder with clip
- ✓ 1 ruler/protractor
- ✓ 1 pen or pencil
- ✓ 1 cutting tool

Steps

1. Cut the tongues of the boots as close to the stitching as possible off the state boots.

2. On the inside as close to the top as possible, use a ruler or protractor for a straight edge. You will want the width to be at least 2-3 inches and the length to be at least 3-4 inches. Make your straight edge on both pieces and cut on the lines as perfectly as you can.

3. On the inside of only one of the boot tongues, make your lines ⅜ inches all the way around. This will be your window or front of the ID holder.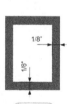

4. Take the commissary ID holder, carefully remove the clip, if it has one, and then pull it apart at the edges. You will only need one of the sides, save the other for when you get another set of boot tongues. Then, cut it to fit the ID holder boot tongue, 2-3 inches wide and 3-4 inches long.

5. Using the center of the tongue that you cut for the window, get the widest part, fold it in half, using your judgment, go in about an estimated length and cut downward and again use your judgment

and curve a J on both sides, that will be for the chain to go through.

6. Decide if you want the ID holder to be horizontal or vertical. Using the back piece and the piece for the chain, center it with the loop on top and sew that down first.

7. Using the commissary clear plastic ID holder and the top frame, close to the inside, sew them together all the way around.

8. Then, sew the two remaining pieces together close to the outside edge.

9. Using the black marker, color the thread to match the black of the boot tongue. Let dry, then wipe really well to remove the excess ink.

MAKE ROSARIES

Required Supplies

- ✓ Cardboard backing from typing or writing pad
- ✓ 6 pencils or colored pencils
- ✓ 1 large bowl
- ✓ 1-3½-foot-long, ⅛ inch or less thick line
- ✓ Coffee (for color)
- ✓ Wax (to seal coffee color on pencils)
- ✓ Several cutting tools
- ✓ Hot water
- ✓ Sand paper (if you can get it), a cutting tool or concrete will do fine, too
- ✓ Glue
- ✓ Sewing thread
- ✓ Empty printer ink cartridges

Steps

1. Remove the aluminum and eraser at the end of all six of the pencils.

2. Sand the color off the pencil.

3. Fill large bowl with hot water and put the pencils into the bowl of hot water (water will soak into the wood of the pencil and help to dissolve the glue holding the lead in the center of the pencil), let it soak for 2 hours.

4. Using an object small and strong enough, push the lead out of the pencil.

5. Carefully cut one piece at least ¾ inch long.

6. Carefully cut five pencils into ½ inch in length until you accumulated at least 64 of the ½ inch pieces (these will be the beads).

7. Carefully cut the edges of the beads to get rid of the rough edges.

8. Take and put all 64 ½ inch pieces and the ¾ piece on the string and tie the ends together.

9. Make a cup of coffee and then dip the threaded beads into the coffee and let soak for about five minutes to ensure that all the beads are evenly coated.

10. Hand the threaded beads up somewhere and let dry.

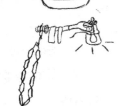

11. Pour some wax into a bowl, then dip the coffee colored beads into the wax, make sure that each side of the beads is coated.

12. Hang somewhere and let dry.

13. Repeat steps 11 and 12 at least two more times.

14. Cut empty ink cartridge into ¼ inch pieces, you should have a least 20 pieces.

Ink Cartage

15. Using the 3 ½ inch long and ⅛ inch or less thick line with some of the ½ inch beads and the ¼ inch cut pieces of the empty ink cartridge. Take the line and tie a simple knot on one end, put one ¼ inch cut ink cartridge then a ½ inch cut bead then continue as follows:

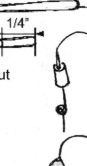

a) Knot on one end of the line.

b) One ¼ inch ink cartridge.

c) One ½ inch bead.

d) One ¼ inch ink cartridge.

e) Ten ½ inch beads.

f) One ¼ inch ink cartridge.

g) One ½ inch bead.

h) One ¼ inch ink cartridge.

i) Ten ½ inch beads.

j) One ¼ inch ink cartridge.

k) One ½ inch bead.

l) One ¼ inch ink cartridge.

m) Ten ½ inch beads.

n) One ¼ inch ink cartridge.

o) One ½ inch bead.

p) One ¼ inch ink cartridge.

q) Ten ½ inch beads.

r) One ¼ inch ink cartridge.

s) One ½ inch bead.

t) One ¼ inch ink cartridge.

u) Ten ½ inch beads.

v) One ¼ inch ink cartridge.

w) One ½ inch bead.

x) One ¼ inch ink cartridge.

y) Tie a loose knot in the end.

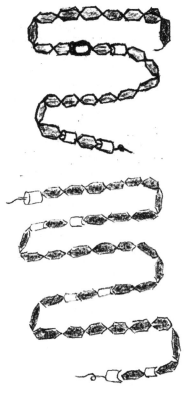

16. Take a couple pieces of cardboard and glue them together, let them dry.

17. Either draw a small picture of Mary praying or glue down a small picture of her in prayer.

18. Cut in a small oval shape slightly bigger than your thumb, make three small holes then put a string through one of the holes then dip into the wax.

19. Hang somewhere to dry.

20. Dip into wax again then hang and let dry. Do this at least two more times.

21. Untie one end of the line and put through the top of the hole on the oval picture of Mary in prayer, then do the other side the same in the hole across from the other and tie the knots as tiny as possible (use fire to singe the ends of the knotted lines).

22. Take a piece of line and tie a knot just bigger than the hole of the pencil then A) slip the line through the hole in the pencil B) carefully pull until the knot slips inside the pencil but the line stays inside the pencil.

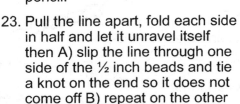

23. Pull the line apart, fold each side in half and let it unravel itself then A) slip the line through one side of the ½ inch beads and tie a knot on the end so it does not come off B) repeat on the other side (you will have to improvise).

24. Pull the two ends of the line apart. Twist and let unravel together. Slip on one ½ inch bead and tie a good knot.

25. Using the same line slip on the following:

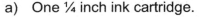

   a) One ¼ inch ink cartridge.

   b) Three ½ inch beads.

   c) One ¼ inch ink cartridge.

   d) One ½ inch bead.

   e) One ¼ inch ink cartridge.

26. Slip the end of the line into the bottom hole of the Mary in prayer and tie a knot (singe the knot with fire).

For those of you who do not know, rosaries are not meant to be worn. They are for prayers. Many people wear them because they think it will protect them or bring them good luck.

MAKE PLAYING CARDS

Required Supplies

- ✓ 1 roll of clear 8-inch-wide tape
- ✓ 2 manila file folders or 1 stack of 54 index card (color, optional)
- ✓ 1 red marker or pen
- ✓ 1 black marker or pen
- ✓ 1 pencil
- ✓ 1 protractor/ruler
- ✓ 1 new cutting tool

Steps

1. Open manila folder and draw a grid of 3 inches by 2 inches. One folder will make 32 cards, two will make 64 cards. If you are using index cards, simply cut them in 3 x 2-inch rectangles.

2. Take the cutting tool and cut slowly and as straight as you can along those lines.

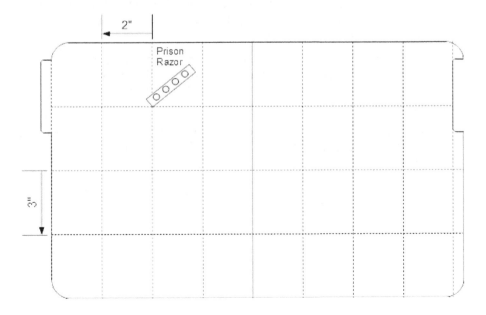

3. With your red or black marker or pen, write the perspective letter or number on the left-hand corner, turn upside down and write the same letter or number. A=1 or Ace, K=King, Q=Queen and J=Jack. Here is what you should have:

Marker		Qty.	Marker		Qty.	Marker		Qty.	Marker		Qty.
A	♥	1	A	♦	1	A	♠	1	A	♣	1
K	♥	1	K	♦	1	K	♠	1	K	♣	1
Q	♥	1	Q	♦	1	Q	♠	1	Q	♣	1
J	♥	1	J	♦	1	J	♠	1	J	♣	1
10	♥	1	10	♦	1	10	♠	1	10	♣	1
9	♥	1	9	♦	1	9	♠	1	9	♣	1
8	♥	1	8	♦	1	8	♠	1	8	♣	1
7	♥	1	7	♦	1	7	♠	1	7	♣	1
6	♥	1	6	♦	1	6	♠	1	6	♣	1
5	♥	1	5	♦	1	5	♠	1	5	♣	1
4	♥	1	4	♦	1	4	♠	1	4	♣	1
3	♥	1	3	♦	1	3	♠	1	3	♣	1
2	♥	1	2	♦	1	2	♠	1	2	♣	1
1	♥	1	1	♦	1	1	♠	1	1	♣	1

You should have 52 cards total if you are playing spades, you will need two jokers. one high and one low (write in the corner a J and under it, write the word "high" and on the other one, the same but with the word "low') *Note: the hearts and diamonds are done in red and the clubs and spades are in black.

When you finish writing out the cards, use the tape to tape the cards up for protection. You can also decorate the other side of the card before you tape it up, that is up to you. Cut any excess tape off each taped-up card.

So, now you wonder, "what about a box for the cards?" Do not worry, there is a solution. (See Make a Box for Playing Cards, next chapter.)

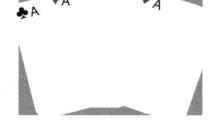

MAKE A BOX FOR PLAYING CARDS

Required Supplies

- ✓ Protractor or ruler
- ✓ Manila folder
- ✓ Pencil or pen
- ✓ Glue

As you already know, the length of the cards is 3 inches and the width of the cards is 2 inches. However, we do not know the thickness.

Steps

1. Use your protractor or ruler and measure the thickness or depth of the deck of cards you have. Write it down. Now, that you have the thickness, you have all the information for creating the box.

2. Take the manila folder and lay it flat and draw the outline of the box on it as shown on the illustrations.

3. Cut along the dotted lines.

4. Fold on the solid lines, overlap the 3-inch sides and glue together.

5. Fold the depth (thickness) on the bottom, which will be approximately ¾ inches and glue together. Let dry.

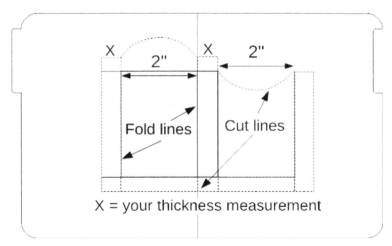

X = your thickness measurement

MAKE HOMEMADE NOTEBOOKS

Required Supplies

- ✓ 3 sheets of drawing pad paper
- ✓ Glue
- ✓ Cutting tool
- ✓ Ruler/protractor
- ✓ 3-inch-wide tape
- ✓ 25-250 sheets of paper

Note: Consider your purpose for the notebook and your financial means. Texas prisons commissary sells one typing pad for $.95 (50 sheets) and one writing tablet for $2.00 (50 sheets), although the quality is not all that great.

Steps

1. If you are using typing paper to make your notebook, you might want to draw the lines on the paper ahead of time, front and back, leaving at least a 1-1 ½ inch on the left-hand side (when you flip it over, the margin will be on the right-hand side). Or you can simply just draw straight lines across the page. It is a personal preference.

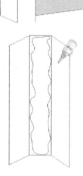

2. Align the stack of paper, and then fold one of drawing pad sheets over both edges, centering the page. Remove the pages, and then draw a line into both creases that were created.

3. Pour glue from the top to the bottom thickly from edge to edge. Align the stack of paper to the glue from crease to crease and press down. Pour glue onto the top page and bottom page, only a ¼ inch from the edge of the stack of paper, then fold the page. Place somewhere that will keep it pressed together. Set aside and let dry

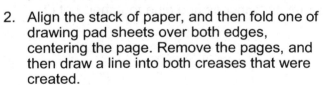

4. Once dry, open the front flap and spread glue out then place the second sheet of drawing pad

paper on top of that glue. Do the same on the backside. Let sit and dry. Once it is dry, cut the excess off.

Optional: glue the front sheet down to the inside of a photo album and the back to the back inside of the photo album. Then, tape it down.

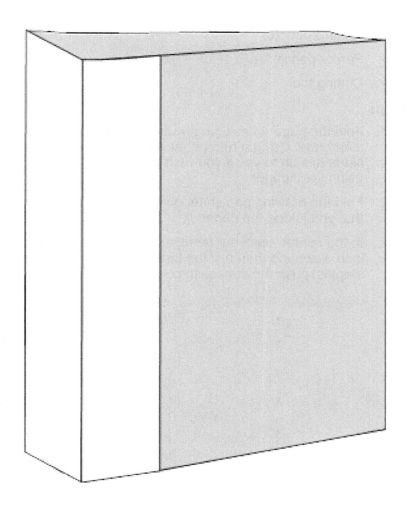

MAKE HOMEMADE MINI NOTEBOOKS

Required Supplies

- ✓ 1 sheet of drawing pad paper
- ✓ 10-20 sheets of paper
- ✓ Sewing needle
- ✓ Sewing thread
- ✓ 2-3 staples
- ✓ Ruler/protractor
- ✓ Pen or pencil
- ✓ Cutting tool

Steps

1. Fold the paper in half lengthwise or widthwise. It makes no difference. Using a ruler, draw lines both front and back. Note: It is up to you if you wish to draw lines if you are not using lined paper

2. Fold the drawing pad sheet over the paper the same way that you folded the paper

3. In the center, use your needle to puncture holes about ½ inch apart and then pull the thread through. Note: If using staples, push the staples through about the same width apart (½ inch) and close staple ends down

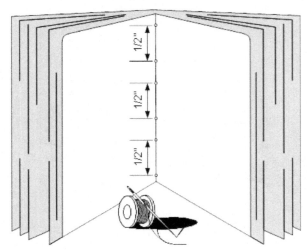

4. Cut the front ends in a straight line, as close as you can.

You can make the notebook as big or as small as you like. Optional: Draw some art or design on the front and label the use for it so you know what is inside.

MAKE ONE GIANT PHOTO ALBUM

OPTION 1

Required Supplies

✓ 3-4 photo albums

✓ 1 roll 3-inch wide clear tape

✓ 1 cutting tool

0Steps

1. Open all 3 or 4 photo albums and remove the plastic spiral by unwinding it outward.

2. Place two of the photo pages' edges together, lengthwise, bare touching.

3. Cut a strip of tape twice as long as the length of the photo pages, place on the center of the two pages as evenly as possible, fold tape over the top and bottom of photo pages, fold together, and align another photo page to the two you just taped up. Tape the third page to the first two like above. Repeat this process until all pages are taped together.

4. Put three strips of tape edges half way over the corner of the edge of the fold down, repeat on the other side, then one down the center, cutting off any remaining excess tape hanging off.

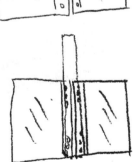

5. Place a strip half way to the center with other edge hanging loose, then put another strip edge to edge and tape to front of photo album. Do the other side the same way.

6. Place the stack of photo pages into the center of the photo album cover, also called the spine or binding of the book. Put a strip of tape all the way around, overlapping the hanging tape from the photo pages, taping it firmly into place inside the photo album cover. Repeat on the other side.

27

7. Place the photo page stack into the center spine of the photo album. Place strip all the way around the photo cover, directly over that strip hanging off the photo pages. Do this on both sides.

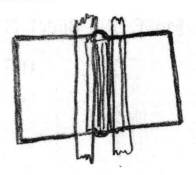

8. Put photos into the photo album any way you wish and enjoy!

MAKE ONE GIANT PHOTO ALBUM
OPTION 2

Required Supplies

- ✓ 2-4 photo albums
- ✓ 1 pair of shoelaces (optional)

Steps

1. Open photo albums and remove the pages by unwinding the plastic spiral rings from the binding of the photo album.

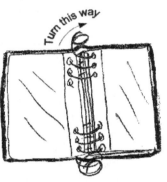

2. Stack the photo pages on top of one another, aligning the holes of the photo pages to the photo album covers' holes

3. Spin the spiral rings back through the holes, if you can. If not, this is where you can use the shoelace or some sort of string to run through the aligned holes. Then maybe do you a little artwork on the cover, make it nice!

HOW TO TUNE A RADIO

Required Supplies

- ✓ 1 triangle head screwdriver/tool
- ✓ 1 flat head screwdriver/tool
- ✓ 1 radio

Note: This radio is Model: CT RAC 70, Frequency: 530-1700 KHZ, FM88-108 MHZ, Power source: AC 120V, 60HZ SW 3155525. Also, your radio must have a tuner box

Steps

1. Unscrew the four (4) triangle head screws, remove the front face frame and front cover lens, then unplug headphones, gently lift the front, pushing towards the back, be careful not to dislodge the light, AM/FM wires, or anything else.

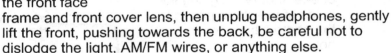

2. The tuner box is a box that has (8) screws. (4) are flatheads and (4) are nuts and bolts. The (4) we want are the top (4) flathead screws. Plug in your radio headphones and antenna, adjust the volume frequency. Turn the dial to a station, (2) screws are for AM frequency and range of clear nearness, the other (2) are for the FM frequency. The screw closest to you is AM and the so is the one to the right, if the clock is facing you. The screw to the right is range and the screw to back is for the alignment band, FM 88-108 MHZ. While making any adjustments, you must turn slowly and listen at the same time. You will have to use your judgment to determine what sounds clear to you. Be careful not spin or turn to screws too fast, because if you do, you will spend even more time trying to return to square one again. Note: Caution, this requires loads of patience!

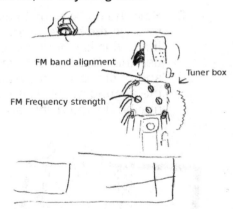

FM band alignment

Tuner box

FM Frequency strength

HOW TO PUT TV ON YOUR RADIO

Required Supplies

- ✓ 1 Radio Model: CT RAC70, Frequency: 530-1700 KHZ, FM 88-108 MHZ 3155525
- ✓ 1 triangle head screwdriver/tool
- ✓ 1 uncoated thin wire
- ✓ 1 2 ½ inch long coax cable wire

Steps

1. Using the triangle head screwdriver/tool, remove the (4) screws from the radio, disconnect the headphones, remove the front lens frame and lens cover. With the radio clock facing you, lift from the front, gently pushing towards the back and turn sideways, careful not to disconnect any wires

2. The tuner box has (8) screws. (4) Flat heads and (4) nuts and bolts. With this model radio

3. "CT RAC-70", there is a silver box in front of the tuner box. Take the thin wire and wrap it around the bar closest to you on the tuner box, pull it snug around the silver box and wrap around the other bar closest to you.

4. Bend the 2 ½ inch coax cable wire into a "u" shape; connect one to the outside of the back nut only and the other to the other nut. be sure to bend it so stays put when you place it on the brass nuts.

Coax cable must touch only the brass nuts →

Wire

5. Reconnect your headphones, antenna, and plug up. Adjust the volume. Slowly, turn the dial and you will get a few of the local stations. You will notice the TV band stations will override the FM band frequency. (Cool, huh?) You may get some stations twice, but it is all right. Also, you may have to jiggle the wire or move the tuner dial slowly in order to hear the stations.

MAKE A SPEAKER

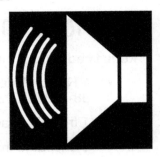

Required Supplies

- ✓ Angel hair wire
- ✓ Dine magnets or textile magnets
- ✓ Casing
- ✓ Glue
- ✓ Coil gauge
- ✓ Box (Illustration board, soap box, tissue box, hard back books, etc.)
- ✓ Head phone cords
- ✓ Typing paper
- ✓ Cutting tools
- ✓ Pencil
- ✓ Ruler/protractor
- ✓ Tape
- ✓ Sandpaper

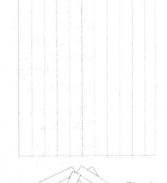

Steps

1. Make the coil

    a. Cut several one-inch-wide x 11-inch-long strips of paper.

    b. Put some glue or tape on one strip, leave some hanging off and begin to wrap it tightly all the way around the pencil end, keep evenly flush. Where the paper strip ends, put a little bit of glue to hold that end the strip into place but enough glue to

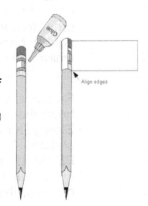

align the edge of another strip next to it flush and wrap it around. Continue this process until the strips are just slightly bigger than the magnet is round (put a piece of tape around the coil gauge backwards then put a strip of paper on the sticky part of the tape).

c. Cut the angel hair wire into 30 feet long. (Some people like to use two wires, which are nice, put for this project, you will use only one. The more you make speakers and tweak them, the more you will learn. This project is one of those times you will learn patience and how to handle things that are very fragile.) Leaving the coil hanging off from the coil and put a thin layer of glue around the strip of the paper that you stuck to the tape. Then begin to wrap the wire tightly so there is no space between the wire wrap, at least 17 times. Then, put another thin layer of glue on top of the angel hair coil then wrap 17 more times on top of the previously wrapped. Again, put a thin layer of glue, blow on it to help glue dry faster.

No spacing between wire, 17 up and 17 down for a total of 34 wraps.

3"

2. Make the magnet and casing

a. The casing will enclose the magnet on one flat side and on the side all the way around.

b. Place a drop of glue into the casing in the center, put the magnets into the casing and center the magnets.

Glue

3. Make the box.

a. Take your box (illustration board, soap box, tissue paper box, or hard backs from books), draw a square, appropriate for the material (meaning to leave room so it will stand on its own), and in the center draw a circle. This should give you about a ½ inch from the circumference of the circle to the lines of the square. Then, draw another square 2 inches from that square, circle inside a square that is inside of another square. Make two lines that cross the other line of the outer square.

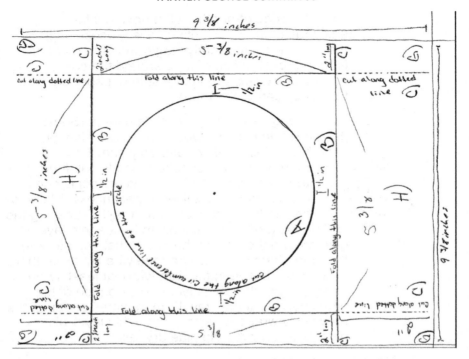

b. Carefully, cut out the circle, and then cut the outer square. Then, those lines that touch the outer square, cut until you reach the 7-inch square line, carefully, fold on the 7-inch square line. The four pieces that are sticking up bend them down, put glue on tip and place under the bigger side wall. Set aside to let dry.

4. Make the cone of the face.

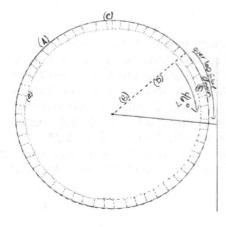

a. Since your circle on your box is 6 inches in diameter, make your next circle on paper about 8 inches in diameter. Be sure to make the center so you can draw a line from the center to circle's circumference line known as the radius

b. Carefully, cut the circumference line then cut the radius line (from the center to the circumference line)

34

c. Put a thin layer of glue about a ¼ inch from the edge of the radius line to then overlap the two radius lines, to form a cone. Give it a little time to dry. Then, carefully, cut slits about ¾ inches apart, about ¼ inch long, around the edge of the cone. Note: you may need to make the slit/cut a little longer, but you will get to check it when you put the cone inside the box to see if cone is flush with the 6-inch diameter.

5. Make the cord.

   a. Take the headphone cord and cut the coating off of about 1 to 2 inches of it.

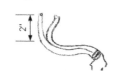

   b. Sand the wires. Be careful, as these will break even easier than the angel hair wire.

6. Make the brace

   a. Take a sheet of paper or two and roll them up tightly, then glue them down so it will not unravel. Make at least two.

   b. Glue them together.

   c. Measure them to fit snuggly inside the back of the box. Remove any excess

7. Putting it all together

   a. Take the cone and glue it to the inside of the box. Let it dry.

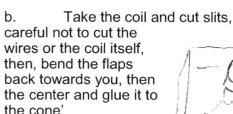

   b.   Take the coil and cut slits, careful not to cut the wires or the coil itself, then, bend the flaps back towards you, then the center and glue it to the cone'

   c. Place the box face down gently; put the magnet and

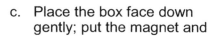

casing on the coil. Put glue on the back of the casing; place the brace on top the casing. Leave it alone to dry.

d. Carefully, sand the ends of the coil wire, then twist one coil wire to one set of the headphone's wires then the other coil to the other headphone's wires'

e. Make sure the radio volume is down, turn the radio on, plug headphone jack in. Slowly, turn the volume up and stand speaker up on the side, adjust the brace using your judgment then put glue on both ends of the brace, turn

radio off or unplug speaker and let the glue dry thoroughly. Once the glue is dry, enjoy!

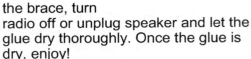

As you tweak with the speakers from cone material to box material even single, double or four wires for the coil, you learn how to make the speakers with more range, better bass, treble, etc. Another thing you will learn is if you boost you radio, you will get better output on your speaker. One other little tidbit: the placing of your speakers also does wonders!

You can also put the headphone speaker on the rim of your hotpot insert cup, place a rubber band around it, then strategically place it so it sounds better and louder in the cell. It won't give you much bass, but it does sound pretty good.

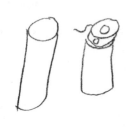

Lockers on the bottom bunk, place under the bunk at an angle about half (½) way back facing the head steel leg of the bunk!

Another option is to cut the top and bottom off a Balsam and Protein shampoo bottle. Cut two (2) "V"s on one end. Place the bottle over the speaker headphones, place a rubber band over it, turn it up and again strategically place it so it sounds really good.

HOW TO TURN A BOWL INTO A TOP

Required Supplies

- ✓ 1 large plastic bowl
- ✓ 1 toothpaste top
- ✓ Cutting tools
- ✓ Pencil

Steps

1. Cut around the top of the toothpaste and clean thoroughly. Save the tube, especially if you're in segregation. It makes for a good slider weight.

2. Draw a line around the bowl, at least one inch from the top of the lid, and then cut along that line.

3. On the bottom of the bowl at the center of the bowl cut out a hole approximately ½ inches in diameter, then unscrew the top off the toothpaste and put it through the hole on the inside of the bowl, then screw the cap back on.

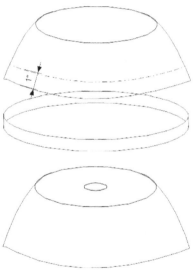

Enjoy your top!

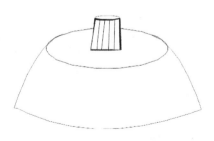

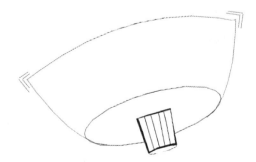

MAKE HOMEMADE DICE

Required Supplies

- ✓ Popsicle sticks
- ✓ Glue
- ✓ Soap
- ✓ Wax
- ✓ 2 balls from roll-on deodorant
- ✓ Cutting tools
- ✓ Pen
- ✓ Sandpaper
- ✓ Domino piece
- ✓ Paint
- ✓ Paper Clips

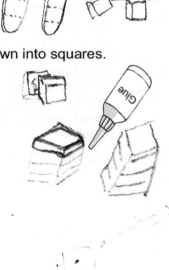

Steps 1

1. Carefully cut the Popsicle sticks down into squares.

2. Glue four (4) of the squares together, set aside, and let dry. Glue four (4) more together, set aside, and let dry.

3. When dry, sand down all six sides until evenly proportioned.

4. Using a pen, make the dots on each side. (1 dot on one side, 2 dots on another side, etc. until all six sides have either dots or a number, 1-6. It does not make a difference.)

Optional: Spray on wax to all six sides to last longer.

Steps 2

1. Cut a bar of soap down (preferable Dial) to evenly proportioned squares, on all six sides.

2. Using a pen, mark the sides with their perspective numbers.

3. Using wax, spray on a layer or two to all six sides.

4. Keep in mind that soap will deteriorate due to being tossed around and sweaty hands. Soap dice will only last for a short while.

Steps 3

1. Carefully cut out the balls out of the roll-on deodorant.

2. Using sandpaper or a rough concrete spot, rub or grind the balls on all six sides until all are flat and evenly proportioned.

3. If you haven't already, straighten out the paper clip and sand one end to a sharp point.

4. If you are using a sharpened paper clip or the sharp corner of a pencil sharpener cutting tool, drill out the perspective dots or numbers into the dice on the perspective sides.

5. Using a pen or paint, color the dots so they are visible.

Optional: Use wax with the ink or paint to seal in the color.

Steps 4

1. Using the cutting tool from a pencil sharpener or a cutting tool, cut the dominos into squares.

2. Sand them down until they are equally proportioned.

3. Using the sharp corner of the pencil sharpener or the point of a filed paper clip, drill out each of the dots to each perspective side.

4. Using a pen or paint color, color in the dots so that they are visible.

Optional: Mix the ink and paint with wax to seal in the color of the dots on the dice.

MAKE SPINNERS TO SUBSTITUTE FOR DICE

Required Supplies

- ✓ Paperclip
- ✓ Empty ink cartridge
- ✓ Back of tablet
- ✓ Pen
- ✓ Ruler/protractor
- ✓ Eraser from pencil

Steps

1. In the center of the back of the tablet, make a circle, leaving a dot in the center.

2. Make a line at the 00, the 600, and the 1200 angle marks, then align the straight edge with the mark and the dot in the center and draw three (3) straight lines inside the circle, you will have six (6) pieces.

3. Take a slightly sharpened paperclip, leaving about an inch standing up, bend the rest into a coil or square, so when you push the point through the center dot, it will stand, and the board will be flat.

4. Push the sharpened end through the hole.

5. Cut off ¼ inch of the ink cartridge and slide it onto the paperclip.

6. Stick a piece of the Popsicle stick or something in one of the cartridges so you will know which end the pointer is, then puncture a hole somewhere on the other end completely through it. Work it so it will spin freely. Place on the paperclip sticking up from the cardboard. Stick an eraser on top but not all the way down, as it will prevent free movement.

7. Mark each piece of the pie, 1 to 6.

Note: If you want, you can create circles with circles and put a center line in each of those to create a multi-purpose spinner.

MAKE A DOMINO SCORE BOARD

Required Supplies

- ✓ Glue
- ✓ Pen
- ✓ Tape
- ✓ Cardboard from box, illustration boards from writing tablet, soapbox, toilet tissue box, etc.
- ✓ Cotton swabs for score markers
- ✓ Sewing needle or pen tip
- ✓ Cutting tool

Steps

1. Cut out two or three pieces of cardboard about 5 ½ inches long and 3 ½ inches wide and glue them together. There needs to be at least a ½ inch thickness.

2. Starting a ½ inch from the top and side, start placing dots under each other ¼ inch apart until you have fifteen (15) dots in the first column. Move over to the next column ½ inch and place another dot and put fifteen (15) dots under to make the second row. Continue until you have six (6) completed columns.

3. On the bottom section, under the six (6) rows, ½ inch from the bottom and ½ inch from the side, put a dot and continue to place ten (10) dots in the row at ¼ inch apart. Then, place a second row directly above it, a ½ inch apart. There will only be two (2) rows of these dots for a total of twenty (20) dots.

4. Number four columns from the outside bottom dot start numbering by fives starting with the far-left column. So, the first dot would be 5, the second dot would be 10 and so on until 75. Move to the second column and start with 80 and go down and the last one will be 150. Do the same to outside columns on the far right, but the outside column will start with 150 and count backwards by five. So, the bottom outside would be 150, the second would be 145 and so on the bottom on the second column, which would be 5.

41

5. The bottom two rows are to be numbered 1-10 each. These two rows of 1-10 are to keep count of the wins.

6. (Optional) Using clear tape, tape the scoreboard up, trying not to wrinkle the tape.

7. Take the sewing needle or pen tip, puncture the holes for the markers to go into. DO NOT go all the way through the scoreboard

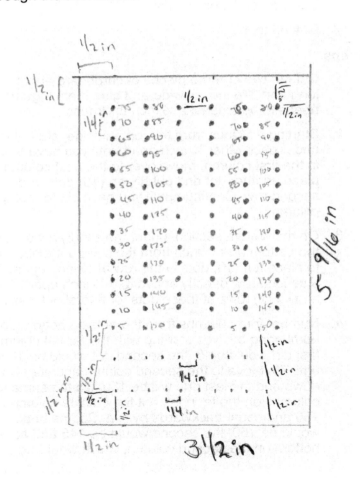

8. Take the cotton swabs or ink cartridges and cut at least (6) ¾ inch pieces. (You can also use ink cartridges cut down to about ¾ inch long pieces). These are your markers. The center columns are for the cotton swab marker pieces.

HOW TO SWITCH LENS FROM
FRAMES TO FRAMES

Required Supplies

- ✓ 1 state provided prescription glasses
- ✓ 1 set of frames of your choice
- ✓ Paper tape, 3-inches wide
- ✓ Pencil
- ✓ Tool to use to remove screws, if necessary

Steps

1. Place a strip of paper tape on top of the state prescription lens, after you remove it.

2. Place the lens of the frames you wish to change into, on top and align the top edges, right on the right, the trace the bottom of the lens.

3. Using the concrete, non-smooth surface (it will feel like sandpaper) and grind down until you reach that line. Remove the tape and put the lens into the new frames. Do the same for the other side.

4. Remove tape and place into perspective places in new frames.

HOW TO WRAP YOUR HEAD PHONES

Required Supplies

- ✓ 1 Headphone band
- ✓ 2 10-foot-long plastic line or other line
- ✓ 2 popsicle sticks
- ✓ Cutting tool
- ✓ Tape

Steps

1. Adjust the inside of the headphones band to where you want it to stay. Take a Popsicle stick and cut it to fit that spacing, wrap one layer of tape around the headphone band and the Popsicle stick to hold it in place. Do the same to the other side.

2. Take one of the ten-foot lines, fold it in half and place the headphones at the top end of the adjustment side into the center of the folded line and tie a simple knot.

3. Make a loop on top, wrap the other line over the top of the line behind the band and into the loop of the top line. Pull tight. Repeat the sequence until you reach the end of the line. Make sure to keep the line you put on top that you want to stay on top with every new loop. When you reach the end, bring both ends together and do a fisherman's knot. Cut off the excess and singe the knot, it helps to keep the knot from coming undone.

4. Repeat process steps 1- 3 on the other.

OPTIONAL:

You can do the same thing to the pieces that hold the earphones or do a single line. Start on one side and tie on to the end, then keep the line either on top during the whole process or the back during the whole process but stick the end of the line through the loop pull tight, make another loop put the end through pull tight make sure that the earphone piece stays in between the line during the whole time.

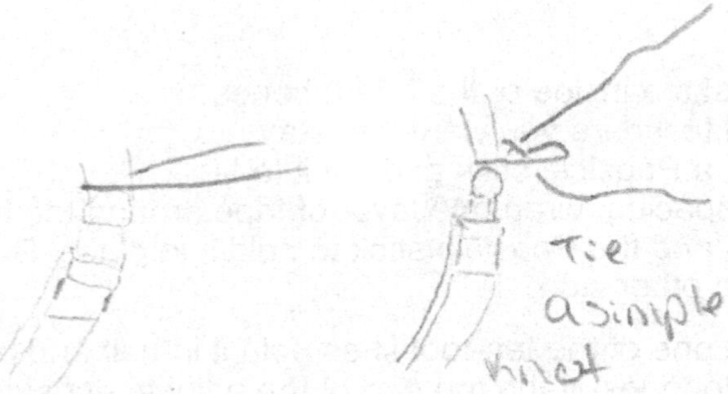

Tie
a simple
knot

MAKE A SLEEVE

For those of you wondering, a "sleeve" in this context is a long envelope with an opening. It has two holes in the top to tie a line on and has a slim width to fit through "rate holes."

Rat holes, yes, are small openings in the bottom corner of one side of a prison door. You can imagine how they got their name.

The purpose of a sleeve is to help to pass stuff to other prisoners and to keep curious eyes (snitches) from seeing what is being passed. Also, it helps prevent losing things or getting them wet.

Required Supplies

- ✓ 1 10"x15" Kraft white envelope
- ✓ 3-inch wide tape
- ✓ Cutting tool
- ✓ Backing of a pad of paper
- ✓ Pen

Steps

1. Draw a straight line, length-wise, 4 ½ inches wide, all the way down. Then, cut along that line.

2. Remove the flap or lick or peel and seal it to the inside of the slender long envelope.

3. Take the backing of the pad of paper and cut two (2) squares, 2 inches x 2 inches, about ¼ inch in and ¼ inch from the top, draw a square that is ¼ inch x ¼ inch, cut that out of both of the 2 x 2-inch squares.

4. At the top of the sleeve (the mouth), about ½ inch down, center one of the 2 x 2-inch cardboard squares, then, trace

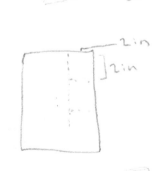

the inside of the ¼ x ¼ inch square. Then, cut out the little squares. You will have a total of four (4) that are a ¼ inch.

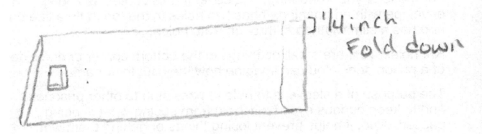

5. Take the side of the white envelope and fold down about ¼ inch then tape the entire white envelope. Be sure to fold tape down into the envelope. Then, align the two 2 x 2-inch square, only one on the outside but align it to other ¼ inch by ¼ inch square hole. Take it in place very well. Then, do the same to the other side. Cut the tape inside of those two sides of the ¼ inch x ¼ inch hole.

That is your sleeve.

MAKE A SLIDER WEIGHT

Required Supplies

- ✓ 1 small chip bag. tube of toothpaste, pouch, or coffee bag
- ✓ 1 staple or cereal bowl
- ✓ Sewing needle
- ✓ State soap bars
- ✓ 1 100-250-foot long line

Steps

1. Depending on the space between the floor and the bottom plate of the cell door, will determine the amount of state soap bars you will need to crush up. It will also depend on the object you will choose for your slider weight. Clean out the item you choose to convert into your slider weight. Crush up the desire number of state bars of soap. Add a little bit of water, smash, and press together until it begins to bind itself. Keep smashing all sides together. Then, put it into the object and smash evenly to the bottom and sides. Continually, test it to see if it will fit smoothly around the whole object under the door.

2. Take about 2 ½ inches to 3 ½ inches of the line and tie a knot into the two ends making a loop. Press the knot into the mouth of the slider weight. Then, sew all the way across above the line leaving some of the loop exposed.

3. At the bottom, press one end of the staple through and press together and slightly open the other end. This is the hook. If you are using a cereal bowl, cut out a piece that looks more like a three-pointed crown. Then, sew into the bottom end of the weight, sewing across the solid flat end.

4. Tie one end of the line to the loop on the weight. Then, tie a loop on the other end.

wrap the line up by putting the loop either on your thumb or pinkie finger and do a figure eight wrapping. Leave about 6-10 feet undone so can pull the figure eight wrapping off your hand and wrap around the figure eight. It also helps to prevent knots.

MAKE A TEMPORARY FIX TO A LEAKING HOT POT

Required Supplies

- ✓ Lighter
- ✓ Eraser from pencils
- ✓ Solder gun
- ✓ Soldering wire

Steps

1. Eraser: Identify where the leaks are, then dry the hot pot out thoroughly.

2. Heat rubber eraser to melting point and melt into each hole.

3. Soldering: Identify where the leaks are, then thoroughly dry the hot pot out.

4. Heat soldering gun, then solder holes with soldering gun and soldering wire.

HOW TO FIX YOUR FAN

Required Supplies

- ✓ Flat head tool
- ✓ Cutting tools
- ✓ Soldering iron (optional)
- ✓ Tape (if you can get it)
- ✓ Paper clip
- ✓ Wire

When a fan breaks down do not despair, there is still hope. Try these three things before you find a way to replace it. In Texas prisons, you do not want to be caught dead without a fan!

There are three reasons that are known for a fan not to work. Well, four, if you count dropping it while waving it around to bring yourself some air relief. We are not going to. It's probably one of these:

1. A short in the cord somewhere.
2. The fuse in the plug blew out.
3. The motor is burned out.

So, when you plug in your fan, turn it on, and it does not work, try moving the cord from the base of the fan and work your way up the cord to the plug. If nothing, pull out your tools, because you now know it's going to be either the fuse or the motor.

Steps

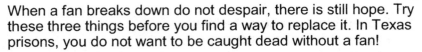

1. Fixing the Fuse: The male prong on these whirlwind fans that Texas inmates pay $22.50 for comes equipped with a fuse which is soldered on one side of the cord. But it is a process to get to the fuse.

   a. Begin by carefully cutting just above the prongs all the way to both sides. Lift up the flap, there will be a hard-plastic box with another lid. Pry that lid up as well. Dig out the filling around both sides unless you get lucky and guess the first-time which side the fuse is in.

    b. Work on removing that fuse. If using a solder gun, solder the wire back to the cord wire. If not, make sure the wire and the cord has a direct connection.

2. Push the wires down inside the box to ensure both sets of wires that are connected to the male prongs and the cord do not touch each other. Replace the lid. Push the cover back down and tape down or string down.

Plug your fan in. It should work. If not, we now know that it is burned out. Your fan is officially only good for parts. The cord is good to make stingers or multi-outlets. The motor has four sets of wires in bundles, which are good for antennas to use for TV or radio, homemade lighters, and tattoo guns (24 volts). The center of the cover makes a nice and tight lid for the hot pot insert cup.

But before you part it out, let's back up a second. Let's just say that it is a short in the cord. You can rig it up so the cord continues to have contact, or you can try this option first:

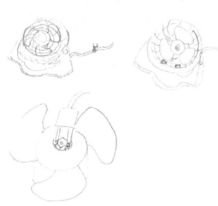

1. Move the cord around the whole length to find the short. Then remove the fan cover, remove the fan cutting tool by placing the make prongs on either side of the nut, hold lightly as you turn the cutting tool to the left to loosen the nut.

2. Using your flathead tool, remove the four silver or gray screws that hold fan motor and switch to the case. Remove the speed switch knob and push the switch box back at its grips. Remove the four screws that hold the fan motor to the back plate. Remove the screw that holds the thermal box in place (optional). just to clean the fan. Use a paperclip,

straighten it out, and push it inside the switch box to the cord pull out the cord. Do it again to the second.

3. Go to where the short is, cut it off, then splice and remove the coating of the wire about one inch exposing the wires. Twist each set, and then push the cord back through the hole for the cord on the back plate, then push the paperclip back into the switch box. Push one exposed wire/cord side into it and pull out paperclip to make sure the cord is snug in the hole. Do the other side.

4. Snap the switch box back into its perspective place. Attach the speed switch knob, plug in the fan and turn it on. If it

runs, then it is fixed. If not, you did all the work for nothing. Either way, you need to replace the screw to the thermal box, then the screws to the motor to lock the motor to the back plate. Put the back plate to the case and put the screws back in. Then install the fan blade and the cover. Never get water in the motor. Just wipe it down periodically, like once every two or three

months.

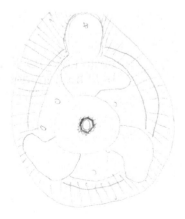

MAKE A HOMEMADE EMORY BOARD

Required Supplies

- ✓ Popsicle stick
- ✓ Sandpaper
- ✓ Glue

Steps

1. Cut sandpaper to fit the Popsicle stick, two pieces.

2. Put glue on the Popsicle stick smooth out evenly. Place the cut sandpaper on the glue on the stick. Let dry. Now, repeat on the other side.

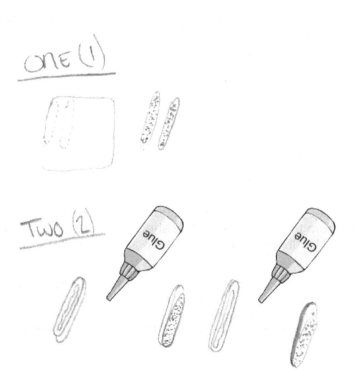

one (1)

Two (2)

MAKE YOUR BED WITH FLAT SHEETS

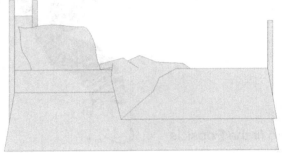

There are several options to choose from, however, it will depend on one's routine, interests, and both physical and mental discipline.

In some prisons, inmates are allotted two sheets, no pillows (this is because they are manufactured to be inside of the mattress). No blankets, except for during the cold winter months or if you are in administrative segregation in high security, which has a cooling system.

If you are one who is meticulous about making up your bed, here are some options when using flat sheets.

After the sheets are washed and dried or exchanged, make sure your floor is clean. Lay the sheet down flat on the floor or remove your mattress from the bunk and lay down the sheet where the mattress was, place the mattress down on top. Using your judgment, align the sheet as evenly as you can from top to bottom and on both sides. Pull the top of the sheet over and then both sides over the top of that about 4 or 5 inches from those corners of the sheet. Pull them tight and into a knot twice. Use three knots, then do the same at the bottom and flip over.

This is the old-fashioned style by placing sheet over the mattress, tuck in the top and bottom, lift each side to a 45-degree angle, and then tuck it in. Place hand against the edge. Fold the 45-degree angle back down and tuck it in. Repeat to the other three sides.

To do a double top off, take another sheet lay it flat, the hem at the top edge of the mattress, lay your blanket on top and smooth them out flat. Align the top edge of the blanket with the top of the hem of the sheet, and then pull back about 6 to 8 inches. Tuck in the bottom, lift the side, and do a 45-degree angle. Tuck in all the way smooth and flat as tight as you can, do the same to the other side.

Another method is after you tie the top and bottom, some people like to use tissue balls and string every 9 to 15 inches to tie the sheet so it stays nice and tight.

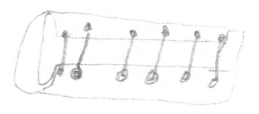

Texas prisoners are cursed to have a cotton mattress, so it gives no comfort or support. Often times, this causes back problems. The mattress can be lumpy, so some people beat them to try and recreate soft fluffiness. This may or may not work. It does not hurt to try.

If you can sew or know someone who can, you can have elastic put into the corners so that the sheet stays on, to eliminate tying altogether.

You could have a mattress slip or cover to slip your mattress into, aka "The Burrito Cover."

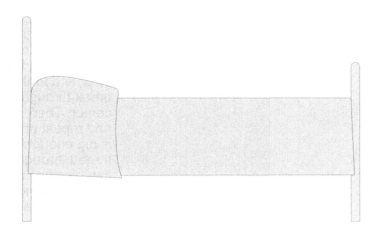

MAKE A HOMEMADE SEWING NEEDLE

Required Supplies

- ✓ Paperclip/snap button with ring
- ✓ Lock
- ✓ Cutting tool from pencil sharpener/several cutting tools
- ✓ Sheet of sandpaper/none smooth concrete surface

Steps

1. If you are using a paperclip, straighten it out and cut or bend until it breaks about 1 ½ inches long. Sand down the end that you broke off into a point. If using a snap button, sand it down on the none-smooth concrete surface until the ring can be popped out. Sand it down until you can pop the brass ring out with something strong enough to dig behind the ring and push it inward and up to get it out. Then, straighten it out and sand down one side into a point.

2. Using the "U" metal of the lock, use it like a hammer on the opposite end of the point to flatten it out, flip it over and continue to flatten it out.

3. If you are using the cutting tools from the pencil sharpener, use the sharp pointed corner, use it in the center of the flat part of the paperclip or brass ring like a drill and hold the needle in place as you twist back and forth, flip it over and align the pencil sharpener cutting tool corner to the small eye and twist a few times back and forth. This is your sewing needle. If using cutting tools, cut back and forth until you break through the center. Then, flip over and repeat until the eye is big enough to slip the thread through. You can also use a staple however using a staple is much more difficult.

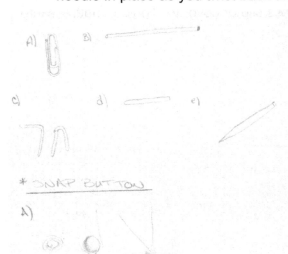

ONE

MAKE SOCK LINERS

Required Supplies

- ✓ Pair of tube socks
- ✓ Hook (staple or paperclips)
- ✓ 2 pencils
- ✓ toothpaste or bottle

Steps

1. Socks are woven together, so, where the elastic bands stop, cut all the way around, flip over and carefully remove the tiny elastic bands without cutting the sock itself.

2. Gently pull on the edges until you remove all the little loose lines. You will end up having four strands to pull two grays and two white, however, it will be one and one. Keep pulling and wrap around your spinner. Tie the one end into a knot then a slipknot, stick into toothpaste, tighten, and then wrap up. When you reach the other end of the line, tie a simple knot then a slipknot, put on pencil. Place the hook in the end of the toothpaste or a loop and hook around the neck of the bottle and unravel about 2 to 3 feet and start spinning. After a couple of spins, roll up, unravel some more and spin again. Repeat until you do the whole line.

3. Repeat with the other sock.

4. Put the two ends together and tie the ends then let unravel. Place under the hook; let it unravel itself, together. Tie a slipknot on the line and wrap up on your spinner. Continue to do this until you have done the whole line. Tie a knot at the end.

When you spin each line, they must be spun in the same directions. So, when you put them together, it will unravel itself in the opposite direction. Then, the line will be unraveled off the spinner and you will push with your thumb and finger for about 5 to 6 hours the pigtails to either end. Enjoy your new line.

HOW TO BRAID YOUR LINE

Require Supplies

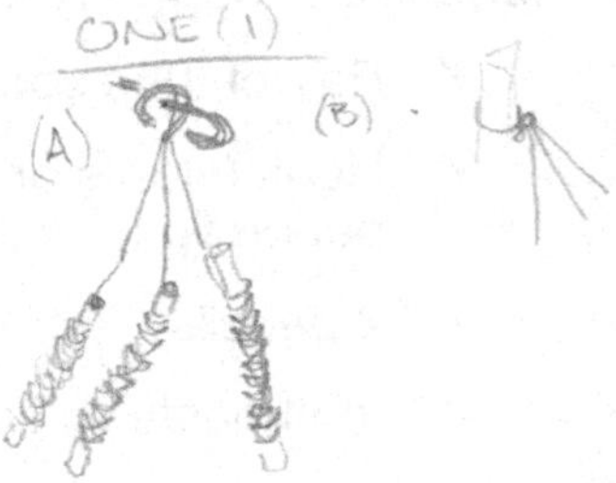

ONE (1)

- ✓ 3 Lines for equal length and width
- ✓ Staple or paperclip
- ✓ Hook (optional)

Steps

1. Tie the three ends together, and then place the knot on the hook or tie around the bar or something that will not move.

2. You must keep the lines tight. Move the outside line over the center, left over center, then right over center. Repeat until finished.

Note: Keep your lines bundled up to where it is, easy to pull looser, but the rest will remain in bundle. As you braid, the line it will braid itself at the bottom and you do not want that. When you to stop to unravel more line, look closely at where you stop and determine which side was down. You want to try and stay with the same side up and the same side down. Otherwise, it was not come out even all the way down.

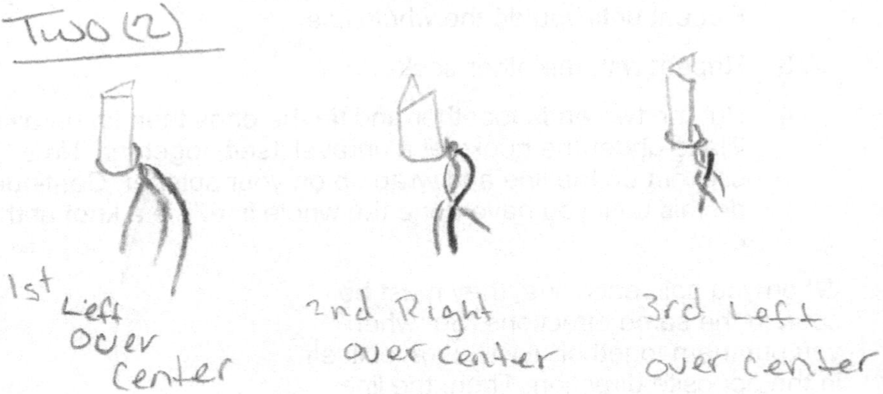

Two (2)

1st Left Over Center

2nd Right over center

3rd Left over center

SEWING PATTERN SHIRT:

Required Supplies

- ✓ Sewing thread
- ✓ Sewing needle
- ✓ Cloth, fabric, canvas, etc.
- ✓ Elastic bands
- ✓ Cutting tools
- ✓ Pencil
- ✓ Bowl
- ✓ Protractor/ruler
- ✓ Zipper
- ✓ Line

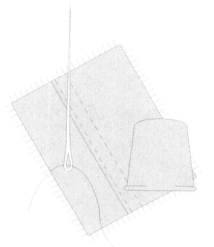

Type of Patterns:

- ♂ Shorts
- ♂ Muscle shirts
- ♂ T-shirts
- ♂ Sleeveless t-shirt
- ♂ Pen, pencil, or crayons bag
- ♂ Bags
- ♂ Beanies
- ♂ Long sleeve t-shirt
- ♂ Ankle socks
- ♂ Pillowcase
- ♂ Face/cell towels
- ♂ Pockets

Steps

1. Use sheets. On one end, cut a slit on the side, then pull the strand out two or three times, follow the line cutting. That will be the straight and even line to follow.

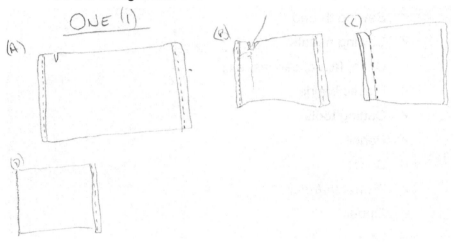

2. Fold it together lengthwise, use the ruler and measure the length for the size wanted. Typically to make 3X shorts, will need to cut the sheet at least 33 inches to 36 inches wide. Then, cut four more slits. Then, pull those threads out, two or three of them. Then, cut along those lines. However, it will depend upon the pattern that you choose to use: a two piece with a slit for pockets; a two piece no pockets; a four piece with pockets; and four piece no pockets.

3. Fold those two pieces in half and cut a slit on one edge in center on one side, remove 3 or 4 stands then cut that line all the way across. Need a curve at the crotch. Look at illustrations for reference.

4. Put these four pieces together lengthwise, align the edges all the way down, then about one inch from the top go down about 23-25 inches and draw an "L" go in about one inch then go up keeping one inch from the edge all the way up. Then at the "L," draw a curve from the edge up about 2-2 ½ inches. Then, from the edge, draw a line down at the angle. (See the illustration) Cut along those lines. If you don't cut the bottom off, they can be turned into pants. However, it

does not matter if it is shorts or pants, choose your desired length so you can hem it later.

5. At this point, this is where you pull out the needle and thread. Thread the needle. Tie a knot into one end. Grab two pieces, at the crotch, fold over twice and begin to sew continuing to fold and stitch all the way up. If you do not fold it over, you will have to come back and do a whip stitch. Do the same thing to the other two pieces.

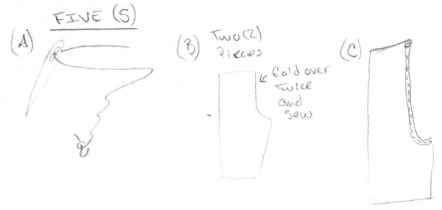

FIVE (5)

(A)

(B) Two (2) Pieces

Fold over Twice and Sew

(C)

6. Put the two together by the inside seam facing outside on both sides. Then, turn the shorts, to the side and fold and stitch down ¼ inch on all four sides including the inseam. All folds will face the same. On the top edge, overlap them so that the rough edges face each other and then sew down about 3 ½-5 inches. Repeat on the other side. Use a pair of boxers to gauge accurately the length from the center crotch seam at the bottom all the way up. Then, fold that top over and stitch into place. There are about three ways to sew an elastic band into the shorts. It is your choice. Just make sure it's 18 inches when folded in half and when relaxed should be about 34 or 36 inches, give or take. You can get bands from boxers to put into shorts or spin lines with.

7. Make sure that the shorts are inside out; put both hands through the band and grab the shorts while sitting down Indian style and pull over your knees fully stretch out the band and material. Thread the needle with thread which is a little longer than the waistband fully stretched out. Do four single stitch lines. You are not a sewing machine or using one either.

8. For the pockets, fold the extra material into four pieces and cut about 6 inches from the edge a straight line down and then in two inches. Then, cut down about 6 inches and across about 4-5 inches and cut up about 12 inches, all the way down. There are four pieces, two for one pocket. Do the stitch leaving the mouth open then come back and Use a whip stitch. Or you can double fold and stitch it. Again, leave the mouth of the pocket open and then flip the mouth of the pocket backwards about a ½ inch. Do a single stitch. Do this to both sets.

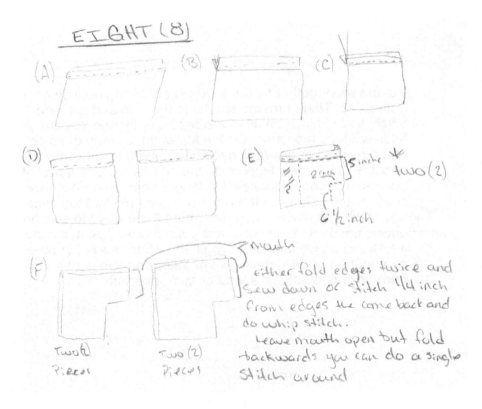

EIGHT (8)

9. Take one pocket and stitch it into the side. Go down and then back up, aligning the stitches to the previous stitches when the band is sewn into. Repeat the process to the other side of the shorts. Put the bottom seam under the pockets together and sew down and back up again next to it aligning the stitches. Do the other side the same way.

10. Decide how long you want your shorts. Then mark it. Fold it in half again and mark it there. Stitch the inside seam. Cut across from mark to mark that has the desired length. Fold twice all the way around. Knot it off. Do the other the same way.

TEN (10)

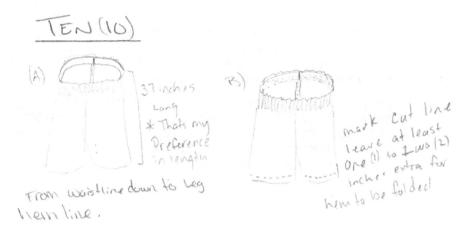

(A) 37 inches Long
* That's my Preference in length

From waistline down to leg hem line.

B) mark cut line leave at least one (1) to two (2) inches extra for hem to be folded

11. Cut a piece of material. Pull out a thread or two, cut the line. Move over about 4 ½ inches across and cut a slit then remove a thread or two, cut along the line. About 6 or 7 inches from the top, pull out a thread or two then cut along that line. If necessary, fold the three remaining sides once and sew them down with a single stitch. On the shorts, check the inside of the band to see which side that the band was stitched together that will be the back. Fold in half front both left and right inside and turn it so the back-left side is facing you. Using judgment, begin to sew in the back pocket. Sew one way then back the other way. Then, on the tops of both sides of the back pocket, sew over and over, going down about ¼ inch and back up. Doing this gives needed strength to the pocket do to the stress of use.

SEWING PATTERN: MUSCLE SHIRT

Steps

1. Decide on the material (T-shirt or thermal shirt). Carefully remove the collar either by pulling the thread out if you know how or by cutting the thread with a cutting tool. The collar comes in handy when making sleeveless t-shirts. Cut along the seam of the sleeves connecting to the shirt or thermal.

2. Fold the t-shirt or thermal top in half. Figure out how tight you want the muscle shirt to be. Cut off evenly on both sides down. Figure out how wide you want the shoulder strap to be. Make sure to leave ½ inch to fold twice and stitch. Remember to always leave room to stitch or fold twice and stitch whichever method you choose.

3. Sew the sides at least ¼ inch from the edge going up and back down keeping the edges aligned. Make a whip-stitch on both sides, then fold together again from the 1½ inch mark and cut downward creating a slight curve until you meet the 13 to 14-inch stitch. Then cut.

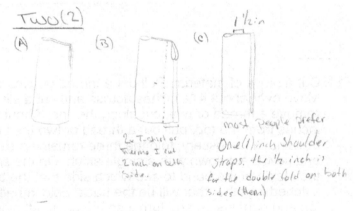

4. Start on one strap, fold over twice as small as you can, hiding the rough edge then sew all the way around. Do the same to the other side.

5. Take the bowl and lay it down on top of the shirt. Go down about 4 to 5 inches and trace the curve of the bowl. On the back, align the bowl's edge to the collar sides, and then push the bowl inward to create a smaller curve, trace then cut

along both of those lines. Fold twice and stitch. Make sure all folds are facing the same side as the inside side stitches.

SEWING PATTERN: T-SHIRTS

Required Supplies

- ✓ Sheet
- ✓ Ruler/protractor
- ✓ Sewing thread
- ✓ Cutting tool
- ✓ Sewing needle
- ✓ Pencil
- ✓ Large bowl
- ✓ T-Shirt

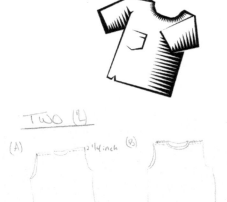

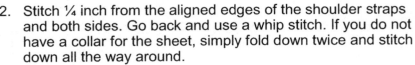

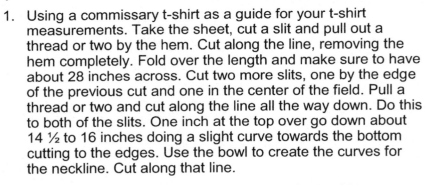

Steps

1. Using a commissary t-shirt as a guide for your t-shirt measurements. Take the sheet, cut a slit and pull out a thread or two by the hem. Cut along the line, removing the hem completely. Fold over the length and make sure to have about 28 inches across. Cut two more slits, one by the edge of the previous cut and one in the center of the field. Pull a thread or two and cut along the line all the way down. Do this to both of the slits. One inch at the top over go down about 14 ½ to 16 inches doing a slight curve towards the bottom cutting to the edges. Use the bowl to create the curves for the neckline. Cut along that line.

2. Stitch ¼ inch from the aligned edges of the shoulder straps and both sides. Go back and use a whip stitch. If you do not have a collar for the sheet, simply fold down twice and stitch down all the way around.

3. Under the bottom of the armpit measure about 25 inches down cut across all the way off. Then, fold twice and stitch it all the way around.

4. Take the extra material fold to where you have the wide and long pieces. Fold them together, lay down flat then place the t-shirt shoulder aligned to the fold and the rough edges at the bottom. Trace the line of the t-shirt down to the bottom of the armpits. Using a straight edge, draw a line at an angle leaving the end wide for the arm. Cut carefully about ¼ inch

to the outside of those two lines. Measure about 10 inches, draw a straight line and cut on that line. Take one of the pieces, realign the edges and stitch from the pit to the edge then whip stitch it. Flip it inside out; bring the edges together make sure when you sew the sleeve on the stitch will be inside when you flip the shirt inside out. Sew it down ¼ inch from the edge as you keep it aligned. Do this to both sides. Fold the ends of the sleeves twice and sew down. Flip the shirt back. You may want to modify and use your judgment as to what works for you and what looks right to you.

FOUR (4)

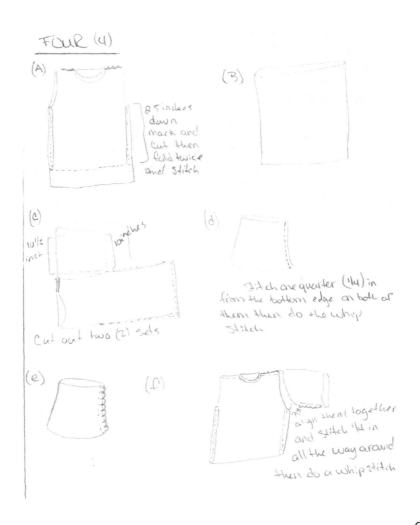

(A)

(B)

8 5 inches
down
mark and
cut then
fold twice
and stitch

(c)

10½ inch

inches

Cut out two (2) sets

(d)

Stitch one quarter (¼) in
from the bottom edge on both of
them then do the whip
stitch

(e)

(f)

bring them together
align them
and stitch ¼ in
all the way around
then do a whip stitch

69

SEWING PATTERN: SLEEVELESS SHIRTS

Required Supplies

- ✓ Commissary t-shirts collars
- ✓ Commissary t-shirt
- ✓ Cutting tools
- ✓ Sewing thread
- ✓ Sewing needle

Steps

1. If you have not already removed the sleeves, do so by cutting carefully along the seam that binds them to the body of the shirt.

2. Fold the edge over twice and sew down. Do the same on the other side. Open one of the collars flat, fold together flat over the edges of the ends. Sew them together. Place the sleeve or arm hole of the t-shirt in between them. Fold down and sew. Do the other side the same way.

SEWING PATTERN: PEN. PENCIL. COLORING BAG

Required Supplies

- ✓ Sewing needle
- ✓ Sewing thread
- ✓ Ruler/protractor
- ✓ Pencil
- ✓ Cutting tool
- ✓ Zipper from jacket
- ✓ Cloth (State pants/shirts or a sheet)

Steps

1. Use the ruler or protractor to measure out two pieces about 9 inches long by 6 inches wide. On one piece, draw a line 1 ½ inch wide on the length. Cut it all out.

2. Take the zipper and cut the thread that holds the zipper to the jacket. Zip up the zipper; bring it down under 10 inches. Cut 11 ½ inches up from the bottom. Take and align the edges of the zipper and the 1 ½ inch strip and stitch it together, ¼ inch from the edge. Attach with a whip stitch. Use the other piece and align those edges of that piece and the other side of the zipper stitch it down and whip stitch it.

3. Place the zipper face down on top of the other piece. Stitch ¼ inch from the edges, keeping the edges aligned. Before you do the final side, slide the zipper back. Do the final stitch and do the whip stitch. Flip inside out.

Optional: Using the same measurements, except forego the 1½ inch cut. Cut out two pieces 9 inches long by 6 inches wide. Sew the cut zipper to the tops of both edges, flip and sew down. Flip the zipper to the inside and stitch all the way around. Use a whip stitch and flip inside out. You have your bag!

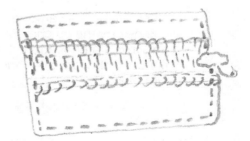

SEWING PATTERN: BAGS

Required Supplies

- ✓ Sewing needle
- ✓ Sewing thread
- ✓ Ruler/protractor
- ✓ Cloth/sheet
- ✓ Pencil
- ✓ Lines
- ✓ Cutting tool

Note: TDCJ used to sell bags of solid material that had a silk feel. Now they sell more expensive mesh bags.

Steps

1. First and foremost, bags have sewing pattern because bags come in all sorts of sizes and are used for various purposes. So for this bag, use these dimensions: 30 inches by 18 inches wide. You can make the bag as big or as small as you desire. Take the sheet and cut a slit on the edge by the hemmed side and pull out a thread or two then cut along that line. Fold in half and measure 18½ inches across, cut another slit, pull a thread or two then cut along that line. Measure down 3 to 3½ inches down, cut a slit and then pull a thread or two them cut along that line.

2. About ¼ inch from the edge of the length, align the edges then sew together. Use a whip stitch. At the bottom, ¼ from the edge, align and sew together. Use another whip stitch.

3. At the top, fold down the edge about a ¼ inch, and then stitch all the way around. Now, fold again ¼ inch. Do a few stitches by the stitched side, push needle about two inches and fold material about 1 to 1 ½ inches down and do you finest stitch work over and over in one spot to lock stitching into place.

4. Run the line through the inside and then tie the two ends together.

5. Finally, flip inside out. Enjoy your bag.

SEWING PATTERN: BEANIES FROM THERMAL

Required Supplies

- ✓ Thermal top or thermal bottom
- ✓ Sewing thread
- ✓ Sewing needle
- ✓ Pen or pencil
- ✓ Cutting tool
- ✓ Large bowl
- ✓ Ruler/protractor

Steps

Using a Thermal Top:

1. Take the thermal top and cut off the sleeves at the seams and along the seams at both sides, use the ruler and pen or pencil mark a straight line under the collar from arm hole to arm hole. Cut along that line. Cut along the side stitches on both sides. You will have to rectangular pieces.

2. Take a piece of thread either a little longer than the material or twice as long as the material. Put the thread through the eye of the needle; tie a knot in one end of the thread. Set aside.

3. Fold one piece in half, pinch at the edge and slip over your head and figure out where it will fit your head comfortably. Then go over at least ¼ inch draw a line up and down. Cut and remove that. Put the two long sides back together align the edges. Thread your needle and start to sew ¼ inch from the edge up, then sew back down. Use a whip stitch.

4. Pull the top down to down to the bottom and the stitch should now be hidden inside. Align the bowl to the top of the edge; mark a line around the bowl. Cut on that line. Sew ¼ inch from that edge one way then

back. Use the whip stitch. Flip it outside in. Put it on and enjoy!

Using Thermal Bottoms (Pants):

Cut on the dotted area indicated

1.   Carefully remove the elastic band and cut along the back seam as well as the front inside crotch seam again on the other inside front of the crotch seam.

2.   Use your ruler and pencil or pen to mark a straight line at the edge. Cut on that line, flip them inside out. Bring the two edges together, the using your needle and thread, sew all the way up then down the other way. Use a whip stitch. Fold down pushing the stitches to the inside hidden from sight.

3.   Bring in the large bowl and pen. Align the bowl to the edge draw a curved line around the line. Cut on that line. Start to sew one way and back the other, at least ¼ inch from the edge and come back. Use a whip stitch. Thermal bottoms will make two beanies.

¼ inch from edge Sew

whip stitch it

SEWING PATTERN: BEANIES FROM SOCKS

Required Supplies

- ✓ Pair of tube socks
- ✓ Sewing needle
- ✓ Sewing thread
- ✓ Large bowl
- ✓ Pen
- ✓ Cutting tool

Steps

1. At the bottom of both socks, cut off the sewn bottom and straight down. Open them, place the socks outside facing each other.

2. Determine how long you want it to be place the edge of the bowl down and draw a line following, the curve of the bowl. Cut on that line. Start on either side, bout a ¼ inch from the edge. It does not really matter. Sew all the way to the other side, sew back the other way sew over and over in one spot and knot it off. Use a whip stitch. Flip inside out and now you have got a sock beanie.

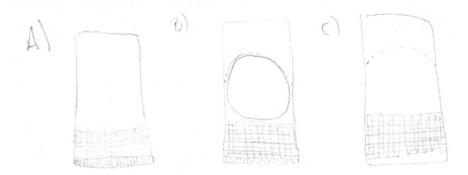

One pair of socks will make one beanie.

SEWING PATTERN: LONG SLEEVE T-SHIRTS

Required Supplies

- ✓ Sewing needles
- ✓ Sewing thread
- ✓ 2 Commissary t-shirts
- ✓ Ruler/protractor
- ✓ Cutting tool

Steps

Take off the sleeve on both of the t-shirts by carefully cutting the thread along the seams. Take one t-shirt and cut into half from the armpits down, cut top shoulder strip. Remove collar. You will have two pieces. Fold in half, align the sleeves, and draw a line going at an angle leaving four inches at other end for hands, the cuff end. Do this to both of them.

Start at the pit bottom and a ¼ inch from the aligned edge and stitch it together. Use a whip stitch. Do this to both sides.

Turn shirt inside out and leave the sleeves inside out (stitches out). Take one sleeve and align it to the t-shirt and do a stitch all the way around. Use a whip stitch. Do the same to the other side.

Flip down the cuff twice then stitch it down. Do the same to the other one. Flip it inside out. Enjoy!

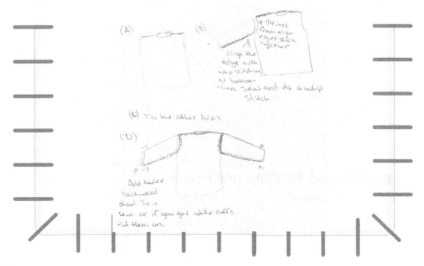

SEWING PATTERN: ANKLE SOCKS

Required Supplies

- ✓ Pair of socks
- ✓ Sewing needle
- ✓ Sewing thread
- ✓ Cutting tool
- ✓ Pen

Steps

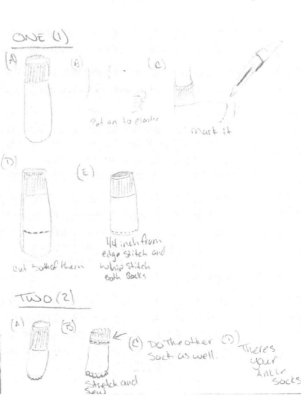

1. Turn socks inside out, put on. Pull the bottom of the elastic up to the bottom of your anklebone. Mark a line in pen ink of where to cut. Take the socks off and cut on the outside of the line, sew the sock. Use a whip stitch.

2. While the sock is still inside out, pull down to the edge of the bottom of the elastic, stretch and sew all the way around.

ONE (1)

(A) (B) (C)

Put on to elastic

mark it

(D) (E)

Cut both of them

1/4 inch from edge stitch and whip stitch both socks

TWO (2)

(A) (B) (C) Do the other sock as well. (D) Theres your ankle socks

Stretch and Sew

SEWING PATTERN: PILLOWCASE

Required Supplies

- ✓ Sewing needle
- ✓ Sewing thread
- ✓ Sheet/state shirt/commissary t-shirt
- ✓ Cutting tool
- ✓ Ruler/protractor
- ✓ Marking object

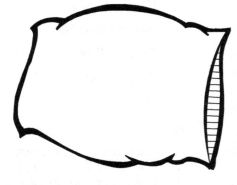

Steps

1. When sewing anything together always leave approximately ¼ inch for the stitching and whip stitch. Make pillowcases for pillows, small enough to fit into a locker. Use commissary shirts, thermals, boxers, shorts, commissary bags, and socks. Use the cotton in mattresses to make a pillow with.

2. Measure the width and length of the material to be used as your pillow stuffing. A good size is 20 inches long by 14 inches wide.

3. Cut your material to the size. Pillowcases are usually rectangular. Remember that the mouth of the pillowcase will need to be folded at least twice. You will need to give at least one inch or more. It is a personal decision.

4. Put two edges lengthwise together and sew together. Repeat on the other side. Sew the bottom together, if you are not using one solid piece of material. Use the whip stitch. Optional: Fold the edges twice and then stitch them together.

5. At the end fold down ¼ inch and sew all the way around then fold down about 1 to 1½ inches and sew all the way around. Flip your pillowcase inside out (or is it outside in!).

SEWING PATTERN: FACE & SHOWER TOWEL

Required Supplies

- ✓ Towel
- ✓ Sewing needle
- ✓ Sewing thread
- ✓ Ruler/protractor
- ✓ Marking object
- ✓ Cutting tool

Steps

1. Take the towel and measure from the hem down the length of about 7½ inches and mark a line all the way across. Cut across that line.

2. Fold the cut edge over twice and sew it down. If the other side is not already sewn down, do so. There is your face towel or cell towel.

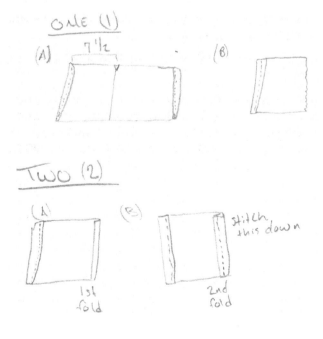

79

SEWING PATTERN: POCKETS

Required Supplies

- ✓ Sewing needles
- ✓ Sewing thread
- ✓ Cutting tool
- ✓ Marking object
- ✓ Ruler/protractor
- ✓ Sheet/pants/shirt/boxers

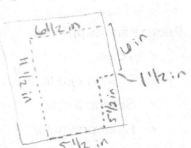

Steps

1. Make a material stack of at least four layers, big enough to fit this size: 6 ½ inches at the top, 11 ½ inches down one side, 5 inches at the bottom and then up 5 ½ inches, then 1½ inches over then straight up. The mouth of the pocket should be 6 inches. Cut the stack on the line or outside the line.

2. Take two of them at the mouth of pocket, fold back and stitch back across the 6½ inch top down the 11½ inch side across the 5-inch bottom, back up the 5 ½ inch side then fold the mouth again and sew over the end. Go back and use a whip stitch. Do the other one.

3. Back Pocket: Cut the material into a 6-inch-long, 5 ½ wide shape.

4. At the top, fold down twice and do a stitch. Fold the sides down and do a stitch. Now, you have got a pocket made for whatever you wish to sew it onto. Notice that you can always make pockets bigger and smaller at your own desire.

ONE (1)

(A)

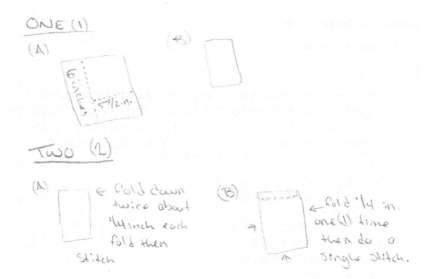

6 inches

5-1/2 in.

(B)

TWO (2)

(A)

← Fold down
twice about
1/4 inch each
fold then
Stitch

(B)

← fold 1/4 in.
one(1) time
then do a
single stitch.

MAKE HOMEMADE RUBBER BANDS

Required Supplies

- ✓ Elastic band

Steps

1. Remove the threads that hold the two lines and bands together. (Sometimes those threads are good for spinning lines so wrap it up on something and put it away for later.) Wrap up the lines on something. You should have about 22 to 24 individual elastic rubber bands.

2. You can do them in any # (1-?). It is recommended to use two to three bands. Align the ends and tie them. Make sure the bands are the same length and tie a knot in the other end.

3. These bands are not that long. Put one end between your teeth and holding the other end in your fingers, hold out to the length that an out stretch hand and arms will go in front of you. Twist in your hands. Using one hand to hold the rubber band, use the other and grab the rubber band near where the crevice of your elbow is, bring ends together. Carefully let the bands unravel themselves together. Tie the three ends together. These are your homemade rubber bands. You can make 1 to 24 rubber bands.

ABOUT THE AUTHOR

Tanner George Cummings, 30-years-old Hispanic male. Serving a non-aggravated twenty-year sentence for escape causing serious bodily injury from TYC in 2007 at the Giddings State School and Home. The halfway point was in 2017 and he will eligible for parole this year as well, but not guaranteed. Tanner is a published author of *The Cell Chef Cookbook and Cell Chef Cookbook II* which is also available from FreebirdPublishers.com or Amazon.com.

Tanner's next book will be *DIY for Prisoners* due out in 2019. He is also working on his first of many word search puzzle books.

GLOSSARY

AC/DC – A unit of force, equal to the force that produces an acceleration of one meter per second on a mass of one kilogram.

Acceleration – To increase the speed of to hasten the occurrence.

Alternative Current – An electric current that reverse direction at regular intervals.

Alternator – A generator of alternating current.

Aluminum – A silver-white metallic element, light in weight, ductile, and malleable, used in alloys.

AM – Amplitude modulation: a method of impressing a signal on a radio carrier wave by varying its amplitude. A system of broadcasting using AM.

Ampere – A unit of electric current equal to the steady current produced by one volt acting through a resistance of one ohm.

Angle – The space within two lines diverging from a common point. The amount of rotation needed to bring one line into coincidence with another.

Approximate – Nearly exact but not perfectly accurate. To come near to in quantity, quality, or condition.

Attraction – The act, power, or property of attracting. An electric or magnetic force that tends to draw oppositely charged bodies together.

Band – A thin strip of material as for binding or trimming. A specific range of frequencies as in radio

Bass – Of the lowest pitch or range.

Bolt – A strong fasting rod, threaded to receive a nut.

Brass – A metal alloy consisting mainly of copper and zinc.

Cable – A heavy, strong rope of fiber or metal wire. An insulated electrical conductor, often in strands.

Can – A sealed metal container for food, beverages, etc.

Cardboard – A thin, stiff paste board, used for signs, boxes, etc.

Casing – A container for enclosing something. An outer covering. A surrounding frame to put in a case.

Charge – To supply with a quantity of electrical energy. The quantity of electricity in a substance.

Circuit Breaker – A device for interrupting an electric circuit to prevent excessive current.

Circuit – The complete path of an electric current including the generating apparatuses, etc.

Cloth – A fabric made by weaving, felling, or knitting and used for garments, upholstery, etc. A piece of such a fabric for a particular purpose.

CM – Centimeter. 1/100 of a meter, equivalent to 0.3937 inch.

Coil – To wind into rings one above or around the other. An electrical conductor as a copper wire, wound up in a spiral or other form.

Conductor – A substance or device that conducts heat, electricity, etc.

Contact – A touching or meeting,

Cord – A string or thin rope made of several strands twisted or woven together. A small, flexible, insulated electrical cable.

Cotton – A soft white substance consisting of the fibers attached to seeds of certain plants of the mallow family. Cloth, thread, a garment, etc. of cotton.

Couple – A combination of two of a kind.

Current – The movement or flow of electric charge.

Cut – To penetrate with or as if with a sharp-edged instrument. To divide with a sharp-edged.

Decibel – A unit used to express differences in power, especially of sounds or voltages.

Degree – Any of a series of steps or stages, as in a process. A stage in a scale of intensity or amount. Extent, measure, scope or the like. A unit of measure for temperature. Math: the 360th part of a complete angle or turn.

Design – To prepare the preliminary sketches or plans for. To plan and fashion skillfully. To intend for a definite purpose. An outline, sketch, or scheme.

Dial – A knob or plate on a radio or television for turning in stations.

Difference – The state, relation, or degree of being different. An instance of dissimilarity. A change from a previous state. A distinguishing characteristic.

Divide – To separate into parts.

Elastic – Capable of returning to an original length or shape after being stretched. Bouncing or springy. Elastic fabric or material rubber band.

Electricity – A fundamental property of matter caused by the motion of electrons, protons, or positrons and manifesting itself as attraction, repulsion, luminous and heating effects, etc. Electric current or power.

Electromotive Force – The energy available for conversion to electric form per unit of charge passing through the source of the energy.

Electromotive – Pertaining to or producing a flow of electricity.

Electrons – An elementary particle that is fundamental constituent of matter, has a negative charge, and exists outside the nucleus of an atom.

Element – A component or constituent of a whole. A substance that cannot be separated into simpler substances by chemical means. The rudimentary principles.

Energy – A source of usable power.

Estimate – To form an approximate judgment regarding the worth, amount, size, etc. An approximate judgment calculation.

Few – Not many but more than one.

Fiber – A find threadlike piece as of cotton or asbestos. A slender filament.

Fiberglas – A material consisting of sending light and images, as around bends and corners through transparent glass or plastic fibers.

FM – Frequency modulation: a method of impressing a signal on a radio carrier wave by varying the frequency of the carrier wave. A system of radio broadcasting using FM.

Force – To drive or propel against resistance.

Frequency – Physics, the number of cycles or completed alterations per unit time of a wave or oscillation.

Friction – Surface resistance to relative motion, as of a body sliding or rolling. The rubbing of one surface against another.

FT – Foot, feet, a unit of length equal to 12 inches or 30.48 centimeters, feet n. pl. of foot.

Fundamental – Of or being a foundation or basis, basic. of great importance. essential. Being of original or primary source. As a principle or rule.

Garment – Any article of clothing.

Glue – A protein gelatin obtained by boiling animal substances in water used as an adhesive.

Hard – A solid and firm to the touch. Firmly formed, tightly. So, as to be solid or firm.

Heat – Energy that causes a rise in temperature, expansion, or other physical change. Maximum intensity in an activity or condition.

Homemade – Made at home, locally, or on the premises.

Hum – To make a low, continuous droning sound.

Illustration – Something that illustrates as a picture in a magazine. An example intended for explanation or correlation.

IN – Inch, a unit of length, 1/12 of a foot, equivalent to 2.54 centimeters.

Insulated – To cover with a material that prevents or reduces the passage or transfer of heat, electricity, or sound.

Joule – A unit of work or energy, equal to the work done by a force of one newton acting through a distance of one meter.

Lead – A small stick of graphite, as used in pencils.

Length – The longest extent of anything as measured from and to end. A large extent or exposure of something. The extent in space.

Loudspeaker – Any of various devices that convert amplified electronic signals into audible sound.

Luminous – Radiating or reflecting light. Clear. readily intelligible.

Magnet – A body that possesses the property of attracting certain substances as iron.

Many – Constituting or forming a large number.

Mass – Physics, the quantity of matter as determined from its weight or from Newton's Second Law of Motion.

Matter – The substance of which a physical object consists or is composed. Something that occupies space.

Measure – A unit of measurement. To extent, dimensions, quantity, or capacity of something, ascertained especially by comparison with a standard. To be of a specified measure.

Meter – To measure by means of a meter.

MM – Millimeter. a unit of length equal to 1/1000 of a meter.

Moist – Slightly wet. damp.

Moisture – Condensed or diffused liquid, especially water.

Mold – A hollow form for shaping something in a molten or plastic state. Something formed or a mold, shape, or form. To shape or form in or as if in a mold.

Needle – A small slender, steel implement with a point at one end and hole for thread at the other, used for sewing. Any of various larger implements for making stitches as in knitting.

Needlepoint – Embroidery on canvas. Noting a lace which a needle work(s) out the design on paper.

Needlework – The art or product of working with a needle especially in embroidery or needlepoint.

Negative – Of pertaining to the electric charge of a body that has an excess of electrons.

Nut – A metal block perforated with a threaded hole so that it can be screwed onto a bolt.

Ohm – A unit of electrical resistance.

Outlet – A point on a wiring system at which current may be taken to supply electric devices.

Pattern – Anything designed to serve as a model for something to be made. To make or fashion after a pattern.

Pencil – A slender tube of wood, metal, etc. Containing a core of granite or crayon, used for writing or drawing. To write, draw, or mark with a pencil.

Plastic – Any of a group of synthetic or natural organic materials that may be shaped when soft and then hardened. Capable of being molded.

Plexiglas – A lightweight, transparent plastic material used for signs, window, etc.

Plug – Attachment at the end of an electrical cord that allows its insertion into an outlet. To connect to an electrical power source.

Positive – Processing an actual force, existence, etc. Nothing or pertaining to the electricity in a body or substance that is deficient in electrons.

Positron – An elementary particle with the same mass as an electron but a positive charge.

Power – To supply with electricity or other means of power. Conducting electricity.

Prong – Any pointed, projecting part as of an antler.

Property – An essential or distinctive attribute or quality of a thing.

Protons – A positively charge elementary particle found in all atomic nuclei.

Protractor – (In surveying mathematics, etc.) an instrument having a graduated arc for plotting or measuring angles.

Radio – A telecommunication system employing electromagnetic waves to transmit speech or other sound over long distance without wires. An apparatus, for receiving or transmitting radio broadcasts. Of, used in, or sent by radio. To transmit by radio. To send a message to by radio.

Cutting tool – A sharp-edged instrument used especially for shaving.

Repulsion – The force that tends to separate bodies of like electric charge or magnetic polarity.

Resistance – The tendency of a conductor to oppose the flow of electric current.

Resistor – A devise designed to introduce resistance into an electric circuit.

Rubber – A highly elastic solid substance obtained from milky juice of various tropical trees or plants.

Ruler – A strip of material as wood that has a straight edge and is used for drawing lines and measuring.

Sequence – The following of one thing after another in chronological, cause, or logical order. Succession or continuity. A continuous or related series, often of uniform things.

Shape – The outline or form of the external surface of something. The figure or physique. to give definite shape to. To assume a fixed or more complete form.

Socket – A hollow or concave part or piece that holds a complimentary part.

Soft – Yielding readily to touch or pressure. Relatively deficient in hardness, as metal. Not rough in texture, smooth.

Some – Being an undetermined or unspecified one. Unspecified one. Unspecified in number, amount or degree. Approximately, about.

Space – The unlimited three-dimensional expanse in which all material objects are located. An available or allocated place.

Speakers – Loudspeaker.

Splice – To unite (two ropes) by the interweaving of strands. To unite (timbers, spars, etc.) by overlapping and binding their ends. To unite film, magnetic tape, etc. as if by splicing. A union, joint, or junction made by splicing.

Split – To divide or separate from end to end or into layers. To burst or break into parts or pieces. To divide or separate into different fractions. The act of splicing. A crack or break caused by splitting. A break or rupture.

Stations – A place from which a radio or television broadcasts originate.

Step – Rank or degrees in a series or scale. To move in steps.

String – A slender cord or thick thread for binding or tying.

Substitution – A person or thing acting or serving in place of another. To put in the place of another.

Supplies – To furnish with what is lacking or requisite or wanting necessary items.

Tape – A long narrow strip of fabric, paper, metal, etc. A strip of material with an adhesive surface, used for sealing, binding, etc.

Thread – A fine cord of a fibrous material spun out to considerable length, used for sewing.

Treble – Of the highest part in harmonized music. Of the highest pitch or range. A high-pitched voice or sound.

Tuning – To adjust (a radio or television) so as to receive a broadcast.

Unit – A single entity. A fixed quantity used as a standard of measurement.

Vibrate – To move to and from or up and down quickly and repeatedly. quiver. (of sounds) to have a pulsing effect. resonate.

Voltage – Electromotive force or potential difference expressed in volts.

Volt – The unit of potential difference and electromotive force equal to the difference od electric potential between two points of a conductor carrying a constant current of one ampere when the power dissipated between these points is one watt.

Volume – The degree of sound intensity. Loudness.

Watt – A unit of power equivalent to one joule per second and equal to the power in a circuit in which a current of one ampere flows across a potential difference of one volt.

Wattage – Electric power measured in watts.

Wave – Physics, a progressive disturbance propagated from a point to point in a medium or space, as in the transmission of sound or light.

Wax – A solid, yellowish substance secreted by bees in constructing their honeycomb. Any carious similar substances especially one composed of hydrocarbons. To rub polish or treat with wax.

Way – Manner, made, or fashion. A characteristic or habitual manner of acting, living, etc. A method or means for attaining a goal.

Wide – Of great extent from side to side. brood. Having a specified measurement from side to side.

Width – Extent from side to side. Breadth.

Wire – A slender piece or filament of metal. A length of wire as a conductor of current in electrical, cable, telegraph, or telephone systems.

Wrap – To enclose or cover in something wound or folded about. To enclose and make fast within a covering as of paper. To wind or fold (something) around as a covering.

APPENDIX A

Clothing Charts

Inches Under Armpits

Shirt Size

20	Med	22
22	Lg	24
24	1 XL	26
26	2 XL	28
28	3 XL	30
30	4 XL	32
32	5 XL	34
34	6 XL	36
36	7 XL	38
38	8 XL	40
40	9 XL	42
42	10 XL	44
44	11 XL	46
46	12 XL	48

Pants Size Measurements

Size	Relaxed	Fits	Fabric B4 Elastic	In.
Med.	12-14 (13)	30-32	Med.	23
Lg.	14-16 (14)	34-36	Lg.	25
1 XL	16-18 (15)	38-40	1 XL	27
2 XL	18-20 (16)	42-44	2 XL	29
3 XL	20-22 (17)	46-48	3 XL	31
4 XL	22-24 (18)	50-52	4 XL	33
5 XL	24-26 (19)	54-56	5 XL	35
6 XL	26-28 (20)	58-60	6 XL	37
7 XL	28-30 (21)	62-64	7 XL	39
8 XL	30-32 (22)	66-68	8 XL	41
9 XL	32-34 (23)	70-72	9 XL	43
10 XL	34-36 (24)	74-76	10 XL	45
11 XL	36-38 (25)	78-80	11 XL	47
12 XL	38-40 (26)	82-84	12 XL	49

APPENDIX B

You Measurement Tool

Okay! So, you don't have a ruler.
Here is a protractor with a ruler built in
and some geometry terms you need to know!

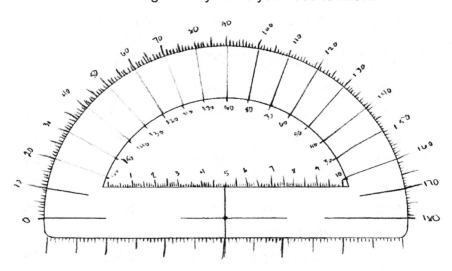

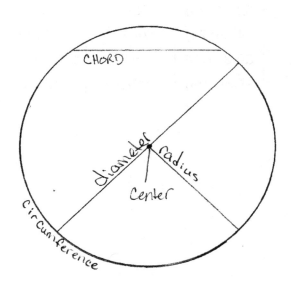

APPENDIX C

Metric Conversion Chart

When you know:	Multiply by:	To get:
Inches	2.54	Centimeters
Feet	.3048	Meters
Yards	.9144	Meters
Miles	1.6093	Kilometers
Millimeters	.0394	Inches
Centimeters	.3937	Inches
Meters	3.2808	Feet
Meters	1.0936	Yards
Kilometers	.6214	Miles

Multiplication Chart

	1	2	3	4	5	6	7	8	9	10	11	12
1	1	2	3	4	5	6	7	8	9	10	11	12
2	2	4	6	8	10	12	14	16	18	20	22	24
3	3	6	9	12	15	18	21	24	27	30	33	36
4	4	8	12	16	20	24	28	30	36	40	44	48
5	5	10	15	20	25	30	35	40	45	50	55	60
6	6	12	18	24	30	36	42	48	54	60	66	72
7	7	14	21	28	35	42	49	56	63	70	77	84
8	8	16	24	30	40	48	56	64	72	80	88	96

9	9	1 8	2 7	3 6	4 5	5 4	6 3	7 2	81	90	99	10 8
1 0	1 0	2 0	3 0	4 0	5 0	6 0	7 0	8 0	90	10 0	11 0	12 0
1 1	1 1	2 2	3 3	4 4	5 5	6 6	7 7	8 8	99	11 0	12 1	13 2
1 2	1 2	2 4	3 6	4 8	6 0	7 2	8 4	9 6	10 8	12 0	13 2	14 4

Mathematic Conversions

Fractions	Decimals	Percentages
1/16	.0625	6.25%
1/8	.125	12.5%
3/16	.1875	18.75%
1/4	.25	25%
5/16	.3125	31.25%
1/3	.3333	33.33%
3/8	.375	37.5%
1/2	.5	50%
9/16	.5625	56.25%
5/8	.625	62.6%
2/3	.6666	66.66%
3/4	.75	75%
13/16	.8125	81.25%
7/8	.875	87.5%
1	1.0	100%

FREEBIRD PUBLISHERS

Thanks for your interest in Freebird Publishers!

We value our customers and would love to hear from you! Reviews are an important part in bringing you quality publications. We love hearing from our readers-rather it's good or bad (though we strive for the best)!

If you could take the time to review/rate any publication you've purchased with Freebird Publishers we would appreciate it!

If your loved one uses Amazon, have them post your review on the books you've read. This will help us tremendously, in providing future publications that are even more useful to our readers and growing our business.

Amazon works off of a 5 star rating system. When having your loved one rate us be sure to give them your chosen star number as well as a written review. Though written reviews aren't required, we truly appreciate hearing from you.

Rate Us & Win!

We do monthly drawings for a FREE copy of one of our publications. Just have your loved one rate us on Amazon and then send us a quick e-mail with your name, inmate number, and institution address and you could win a FREE book.*

FREEBIRD PUBLISHERS
Box 541
North Dighton, MA 02764

www.freebirdpublishers.com
Diane@FreebirdPublishers.com

Sample Review Received on Inmate Shopper

★★★★★ **Everything a prisoner needs is available in this book.**
June 7, 2018
Format: Paperback

A necessary reference book for anyone in prison today. This book has everything an inmate needs to keep in touch with the outside world on their own from inside their prison cell. Inmate Shopper's business directory provides complete contact information on hundreds of resources for inmate services and rates the companies listed too! The book has even more to offer, contains numerous sections that have everything from educational, criminal justice, reentry, LGBT, entertainment, sports schedules and more. The best thing is each issue has all new content and updates to keep the inmate informed on todays changes. We recommend everybody that knows anyone in prison to send them a copy, they will thank you.

* No purchase necessary. Reviews are not required for drawing entry. Void where prohibited. Contest date runs July 1 - December 31, 2018.

Freebird Publishers

Presents A New Cookbook

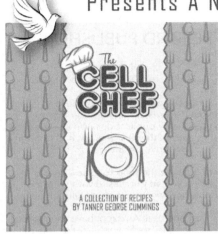

A COLLECTION OF RECIPES
BY TANNER GEORGE CUMMINGS

You will find these scrumptious recipes and more...

Refried Beanie Chicken Winnies

Slightly Sweet Nuttier Chicken

Chipotle Chicken-n-Ranch Burritos

Ted's Po`boy BBQ Crunch

Caffeine-Cino Rush

Sweet Vanilla Sin Coffee

Margaret's Non-Alcoholic Strawberry Margaritas

Charlie's Butterscotch Brownies

Dream Bar Cake

Are you eating the same thing day in and day out? Tired of the same boring, bland tasting food? Are your meals lacking flavor and originality? Then our Cell Chef Cookbook will hit the spot!

The Cell Chef Cookbook is filled with hundreds of fantastic recipes, that can be simply made with everyday, commonly sold commissary/store foods. Every recipe has been tried and thoroughly tested. Loved by everyone.

In the Cell Chef Cookbook the recipes are divided into four sections:

√ **Meals and Snacks**

√ **Sauces, Sandwich Spreads, Salsa and Dips**

√ **Drinks**

√ **Sweet Desserts**

The Cell Chef Cookbook, has an extensive Glossary and Index, created to assist you in the process of your preparations and leading to the pleasure of enjoying these wonderful, tasty dishes.

The Cell Chef Cookbook's recipes have each been organized with a list of all the needed ingredients, and easy-to-follow directions on how to make them to perfection.

Food is essential to life; therefore, make it great.

The CELL CHEF Cookbook

Only $13.99

Plus $5 S/H with tracking

Softcover, Square 8.25" x 8.25",
B&W, 183 pages

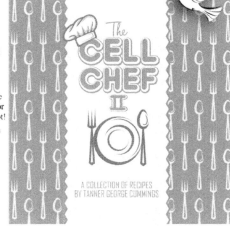

Penacon is owned and operated by Freebird Publishers, your trusted inmate service provider.

Penacon.com dedicated to assisting the imprisoned community find connections of friendship and romance around the world. Your profile will be listed on our user-friendly website. We make sure your profile is seen at the highest visibility rate available by driving traffic to our site by consistent advertising and networking. We know how important it is to have your ad seen by as many people as possible in order to bring you the best service possible. Pen pals can now email their first message through penacon.com! We print and send these messages with return addresses if you get one. We value your business and process profiles promptly.

To receive your informational package and application send two stamps to:

Box 533
North Dighton, MA 02764

Penacon@freebirdpublishers.com
Corrlinks: diane@freebirdpublishers.com
JPay: diane@freebirdpublishers.com